Praise for "Thoughts to Ponder," the blog behind *Echoes of Your Choices.*

"Sharon Dillon's 'Thoughts to Ponder,' a blog put up regularly on her website, is designed to give encouragement to the anxious, old wisdom to the young and foolish, and happy thoughts to those in sorrow. A gifted, humorous writer, Dillon's words, often drawn from personal experience, offer warmth, kindness and generosity. "Thoughts to Ponder" seeks to give a spiritual lift. It entertains as well."
-Barbara N. McLennan, author of *Reagan's Mandate, The Wealth of Jamestown,* and *The Wealth of Virginia.*

"It's good to see Sharon's collection. She has been laboring to find wisps of wisdom to share with a small audience who recognize her talent. Now she can share these with a broader audience who can benefit from her search for truth. A book to turn to, and return to, for comfort and joy."
-Jack Lott, column author, "Inside the Looking Glass."

"Great material to put into a book. True wisdom that you can hold in your hands."
-Linda Bargo, Wisconsin reader.

"Sharon writes with a unique voice, so friendly, it makes one feel we are all in this life together. I come away uplifted and rewarded. I would know her prose anywhere. A wonderful writer."
-John Atkinson, author of *Timekeeper.*

"Her wisdom from life's experiences is success-fuel for anyone who desires to know more of life's secrets and create the life they dream of living."
-Alice Hertzler, MSW

"Sharon's blog entries provide lessons in life. You can always be thankful for a new lesson learned from a writer who advises us always to keep a positive attitude!"

-Linda Grove, faithful reader of "Thoughts to Ponder."

Echoes of Your Choices

By Sharon Dillon

Please visit author website at https://energywriter.me/

Dedication and Acknowledgements

For Dan, Linda, and Sarah, who taught me how to be a better person and parent. They have become adults who make their mother proud. Linda and Sarah guide me in my daily life. Dan guides from the heavenly realm.

Thank you to all my teachers over the years. Each of you has shown me the way to live in peace, love and joy. I won't list your names. You know who you are.

On April 2, 2013 Rev. Angela Peregoff, one of my spiritual teachers, retired from posting her "Morning Blessings" blog and moved on to other projects. I greatly miss her daily messages packed with wisdom and love. Her message that morning moved me to attempt something I had never done before: I have tried to follow in her footsteps. I do not have the same credentials as she, but I do have many years of the bumps and lumps of life as the discovery of ways of attaining peace, love and joy. My goal is to share some of those experiences and "light bulb moments" with you.

You can find my posts at http://energywriter.me "Laugh your way to Peace, Love and Joy." Click on the tab, "Thoughts to Ponder." Your feedback is the most important feature of "Thoughts to Ponder." That is the only way I'll know if I am providing you spiritual nourishment or if I'm just typing for fun. Each post has a comment section at the bottom.

This book is a collection of my "Thoughts to Ponder" over the past three years: short essays in which I describe what has helped me make peace with my world. I hope they will help you too.

Sharon Dillon
June, 2016

Table of Contents   Page

Chapter One: An Introduction of All Are One

ALL FITS TOGETHER

"When we try to pick out anything by itself, we find it hitched to everything else in the Universe." -John Muir

Sometimes we feel alone in the world, or we wish we were because everyone drives us crazy. Our Higher Power did not design us that way. We are made to be social beings who need each other. Our world functions well when every person is doing what he or she is meant to do.

This brings up a couple of questions. The first is: How do we know what we are meant to do? Some people know from the time they are small children. What they are meant to be is apparent in their words and actions. Others of us stumble around wondering what our job is. Some of us are unwittingly doing that job. Others follow the path that a parent or teacher lays out for them. Often people seek spiritual teachers looking for direction. Sometimes they find it, sometimes not.

The other question is: If we're all doing what we are supposed to do, why is the world such a mess? This is harder to answer. I don't claim expertise, just experience. Some people block out their calling and spend the rest of their lives trying to make everyone else as miserable as they are. Some others, people we might call villains or mass murderers, for example, are actually following their paths.

We learn from experience. One of the harshest lessons is to learn compassion by seeing people suffer. To use an overused example, World War II taught us about compassion and bravery. We need to remember that prior to our entry into the war, the United States contributed to the suffering in several ways. By examining history and today's world events, we can see how every action has a reaction. We just need to open our eyes to see it.

Let's also think about the rest of our world. A simple example is the grass in our yards. It's a nuisance to mow and rake, but it holds

1

down the soil so we don't have another Dust Bowl. Grass is also home to small bugs and worms that feed birds and other creatures. Additionally, those worms aerate our gardens so that our vegetables grow, thus allowing us to nurture our bodies.

Recently we enjoyed a full moon eclipse, often called a "blood moon" because the dust and light in the atmosphere create a reddish color. We're expecting three more "blood moons" over the next year. Some people say that these events predict disaster. To others, this is just an interesting phenomenon.

If we want to prove the disaster-predictors wrong, we must not just realize, but feel, the connectedness among humans, animals, plants, water and air. Only by allowing ourselves to follow a path that connects all on our Earth, not just our families or neighborhoods, will we be able to avoid danger to us all. This attitude shift must occur across the world. I know, this seems like "pie in the sky" thinking.

We *can* affect actions across the world each day by asking our God/Spirit/Higher Power for peace, love and joy for all on this planet.

Spirit, thank you for the bounty, beauty, peace, love and joy that you give us each day. We pray that all people and other beings on Earth enjoy and are grateful for your gifts. We know that you provide the sun and rain for the just and the unjust, which is the only way we can live our human experience. We long to see all people surrounded by peace, love and joy and know that you will provide that bounty.

WHAT GOES AROUND

"Here is God's purpose – for God, to me it seems, is a verb not a noun, proper or improper." -R. Buckminster Fuller

Why are we here? What is our purpose? What is God's purpose?

Fuller explains it so succinctly that I could stop right here. But, I won't, and you know it. I believe, like Fuller, that God is a verb. God may or may not be an entity. God is the way we act and speak. Are we kind to others and ourselves? Then we are God. Every kindness done with a glad heart is God.

Oprah Winfrey explains it like this: "The energy you create and release into the world will be reciprocated on all levels. Our main job is to align with the energy that is the Source of all energies and to keep our frequency tuned to the energy of love..." *

We experience what we put out in the world. In other words, what goes around, comes around. Have you noticed that when you smile, other people smile at you? When you frown, others frown at you? What an easy concept to understand and practice!

Many of us will say, "What about all the horrible things that happen in the world?" The same concept applies here: "The energy you create and release into the world will be reciprocated on all levels." These people are not tuned to the frequency of love, so they do not experience love coming to them.

The decision is ours. We can either choose our path of peace, love and joy, or not.

Spirit, thank you for teaching us that God is a verb, rather than a noun. That reminds us to act and speak in a way that we think a Higher Power would.

*"O, the Oprah Magazine," November 2013, pg. 172

3

Chapter Two: Seek Peace

LET GO, MOVE FORWARD

"Give up the need to know what happens tomorrow. Just be fully present and appreciate all that is in your life right now."- Carolyn Myss*

Worry kills us. Doctors and spiritual leaders have been telling us this for decades. Yet, most of us cannot give up the need to know. Many of us are able to give up some of what we need to know. A few have been able to almost completely release that need. Their names are Jesus, Buddha, Quan Yin, and Mohandas Gandhi, among others, but even they found it difficult to give up the need to know. Don't believe me? Read their life stories.

Where does that leave the rest of us? Usually, it leaves us struggling to give up the need to know and stressing about what we can't release. What do we do about it? Usually we worry some more because we can't let go of that need to worry.

Everyday worries include our health, families, budget, city, state, nation, and our response to international events. We can do things to improve controllable personal issues, such as health, family relationships and budget. We can eat properly, exercise, and sleep more hours. But we cannot control the aging process or change our genetic weaknesses.

Are we feeling well today?

We know the steps: eat right, exercise, sleep well and love much. Are the children safe and healthy today? We can teach our children how to eat properly and to spend more time outside pursuing physical activities. We can give them a moral code, encourage them to do well in school, and hope for the best. What we can't do is to assure their future health or change their future decisions and actions. We can only control how we act if our dreams for our children collapse when they choose a different path than what we envisioned for them.

Do we have income today?

We can get a part-time job or reduce budget wants to only actual needs. We can't control our company's possible merger or wholesale lay-off, only our reactions to those events.

The rest is beyond our control. Completely beyond our control. We can write letters to express our view on various issues, and we can speak up at city council or school board meetings, but we cannot control what actions the decision makers make or how it might affect us.

We can only control our response to those events. We can respond compassionately to disasters. We can send money to those organizations whose mission is to provide assistance. We can send peace, love and joy to those whose homes are not safe. What we cannot control is how our donated money is spent or what happens to those in war zones.

All of these words are a long way to express what Bobby McFerrin said more succinctly in a song that made our heads bob as we drove down the highway, singing along with him:

"Don't worry. Be happy."

*January 2013, "O, the Oprah Magazine."

STAY IN TODAY

"Breathing in, I calm my body. Breathing out, I smile. Dwelling in the present moment, I know this is a wonderful moment."-Thich Nhat Hanh

What a simple truth, yet so hard to live! Most of us can only live in the present for a few moments. Then, all too soon, thoughts worm their way into our brains: Today I must accomplish these ten tasks. I think I'll make a stew for supper. Oh, relatives are visiting on Sunday; I must clean the guest room and get extra groceries. And so it goes; anxiety building with each thought.

How do we stay focused on the present moment, enjoying it, savoring it, living it? Each time we realize that we are focusing on the potential future and all the work we have to do before we get there, we can do exactly what Thich Nhat Hanh suggests above: We can breathe. As the calm settles over us, we can thank Spirit for our feeling of peace. With practice, we'll experience more of these precious moments.

There is that dreaded word, "practice," again. We have to practice playing the piano. We have to practice a new task. We have to practice breathing. We have to practice gratitude. We must practice to see not how far we have to go to reach perfection, but how far we have progressed since we started.

Spirit, I thank you for this new day, this beautiful day, filled with new experiences. Some will be daunting. Some will be a pleasure. If I start feeling overwhelmed, please remind me to breathe deeply, smile and enjoy the moment. Knowing that this is so, I thank you for each lesson learned.

ACCEPTANCE IS PEACE

"Acceptance of the world on the universe's terms is the only thing that can lead to peace." -Zora Neale Hurston

Acceptance is a multi-edge sword. In the "Serenity Prayer," we ask to be able to accept those things we cannot change. But we also need to accept the things we can change and to accept gifts that come our way, no matter how disguised they are.

Eventually, if we're open to guidance, we learn that some people will never be who we want them to be, no matter how we try to change them. We can't change the weather, political events or someone's health. Those are the circumstances implicit in the Serenity Prayer.

We also have to accept who and what we are before we can change ourselves. That sounds backwards, but it's true. If we go around saying, "I'm overweight," we continue to attract that which we don't want. We will constantly see cookies as irresistible and exercise as something to be endured. We will constantly see ourselves as less than the perfect people we are intended to be.

If we can accept that we are overweight and look at the gifts behind it (protection from people we don't like; isolation to avoid facing our fears; an excuse to not get out and walk), we can see that those things appearing to be gifts are hindering us from pursuing our goals. If we don't pursue our goals, we can't fail. Sounds like a winning situation, but it keeps us sad and disappointed in ourselves.

This step is not easy. After 30, 40, or 50 years of saying, "I'm fat, and I'll never find someone to love me," we believe that this is so. Trying to accept that, "I'm fat today, but it is not a permanent situation; even if it is, someone who is perfect for me can see through the fat to my worthiness," requires gut-wrenching effort.

Each time we look in the mirror and repeat that mantra, it feels like a lie. But if we say it often enough and trust that it just may be true, we will eventually accept that we are worthy of being our best selves. We may go to the store and buy a new outfit just because we want to look our best, no matter what we weigh. Accepting ourselves as we are (beautiful, sexy, kind, generous, smart, etc.) gives us permission to change, if that is what we want. Cookies will be less desirable. The gym will seem less onerous.

We must also be conscious of the *way* we receive gifts, whether these be verbal or physical. Possibly when someone tells us we look nice, we respond by saying, "My hair doesn't look right today." Perhaps we've been taught that we should say, "Oh, you shouldn't have," or "That is too expensive for me." Those phrases may seem to sound humble, but it is telling the giver, "You really shouldn't have. I don't deserve a gift." For them, it takes the joy out of giving.

Reverse the situation in your mind. See yourself in a store a few days before your friend's birthday. You see an item that you know your friend has been wanting for a long time. It's on sale, so you buy it. You wrap it in gift paper and add a big bow. You feel proud that you've done something special for your friend.

On the big day you present the gift to your friend who says, "Oh, this is too much. You shouldn't have spent this much money on me." How do you feel? What do you say?

Whatever gifts come our way, whether they are smiles, hugs, time, or an expensive item, we should accept them with gratitude. After a while, we'll begin to thank Spirit for the gifts of sun, rain, flowers, and children.... as we gratefully accept our perfect world.

Spirit, today I thank you for all gifts, even the ones I don't like. The ones that make me look inside are painful, but they teach me what I need to learn. I choose to look at every moment as a gift. You have made it so, and so it is.

TRUST RATHER THAN FEAR

"What loneliness is more lonely than distrust?" -George Eliot

Trust is a word that is loaded with emotions like fear, anger, hope and expectation. Volumes have been written about this subject. What more is there to say? Let's try to define trust through ordinary examples.

Trust is:

- believing our children will be safe at school.
- believing that our spouses will be loyal.
- believing that our government will resolve its issues and get on with the process of governing.
- believing that we will be able to pay our bills when they are due.
- believing that we ourselves have the knowledge and strength to do what needs to be done, no matter what else happens.

Did you notice that the list above uses the word, "believing," not, "hoping?" Have you noticed that fear and distrust are synonyms? We feel trust through a knowing, deep in our souls.

We are taught from a very young age to distrust almost everything: teachers, neighbors, strangers, dogs, dark, insects, government, and other religions. This list could go on for pages. We all know what our fears are. Many of these are valid and should be respected. We can't change what will happen "out there," so a healthy sense of protecting oneself is vital.

What we don't know is how to move from fear to trust. This requires a major change in the way we see the world around us, and the movement away from fear is often slow and incremental.

I can recall a time when I told my friends, "I refuse to live in fear." That statement changed my life. I opened my curtains, walked around the neighborhood, and went out to local events. These changes took a few months, but it opened the world to me. Eventually, I began taking larger steps into the world of trust, and I am still learning that it's okay to explore the larger world and to take risks.

We can only let go of fears when we begin to trust ourselves to make the right decisions, to do the right things, to love fully, and to feel endless gratitude. If we make what seems to be a mistake, we trust ourselves to resolve the situation. We no longer need someone else to tell us what to do next.

What you choose to trust is up to you. You can trust your Higher Power, your mind, your instinct. It doesn't matter, because all three are the same. All three will protect you or encourage you to move forward.

Spirit, I know that my fears and mistrust are preventing me from living my life to the fullest. They prevent me from being the best person I can be. I turn those thoughts over to You right now, right here. I trust that You will fill me with knowledge, strength and trust in myself. That gift is mine this very instant, because You have promised it in all the holy writings. And I trust You to keep your promises.

FORMULA FOR HAPPINESS

Minimum Expectations + Maximum Effort = Happiness

Many of us expect that our happiness or well-being will come the effort of other people. We go through life thinking that all we need to do is show up and events will make us happy.

An example: We get up in the morning feeling crabby. So we make a pot of coffee expecting that the caffeine will make us cheery. Instead, it just makes us a little more awake, but we are still crabby. We begin our commute to work believing that being out in the fresh air will make us happy. But we have our windows rolled up because the air conditioner is on. And there's a traffic jam on the interstate. We fuss and fume and finally arrive at work just to face a reprimand from our supervisor for being late. By this time, we aren't just crabby but also convinced that the world is out to bring us to our knees. Our scowls prevent our co-workers from greeting us, much less make us attempting to make us happy.

What if we turn that concept around and realize that our happiness comes from within us and that the rest of the world is there for us to enjoy? Let's try the same scenario a different way:

We get up in the morning feeling crabby, so we make our coffee and jump in the shower, knowing that feeling clean improves our outlook. We walk to our car thanking God for another beautiful day. We also thank nature for surrounding our home with beauty. Our drive goes well until we get to the interstate and become enmeshed in the aforementioned traffic jam. We rummage through our cds and find one that plays soothing music or, perhaps, a motivational message. Since we're not moving, we listen carefully rather than working up a good-sized ball of anger. Finally, we arrive at work. First, we seek our supervisor and explain why we are late and offer to make up the time at the end of the day. He/she agrees, and then we head to our cubicle smiling and wishing good-morning to our co-workers.

In the second example, we made an effort to be happy, to be responsible, and to greet our co-workers. We took responsibility for our own happiness. We did not expect that other people and things would make us happy.

Maximum effort + Minimum expectations = Happiness!

Spirit, thank you for this day that is mine to enjoy or endure. I choose to go forward doing my best work and making an effort to put a smile on someone's face. I choose to be happy, aware, and in the moment. I choose to be the best me I can be.

FEAR OR PEACE

"In times of unrest and fear, it is perhaps the writer's duty to celebrate, to single out some of the values we can cherish, to talk about some of the few warm things we know in a cold world." - Phyllis McGinley

Everywhere I look I see fear and anger on people's faces. Some people are angry that we have a government that can't seem to function. Others fear that they may not receive pay checks and will not be able to survive this contentious time. I'm not pointing fingers; rather, I'm addressing our part in this confusion.

Our part? Are you crazy? What did we do to deserve this mess?

Yes, our part. When we feel fear and anger, those emotions spread far beyond us - to our families, neighbors, co-workers, and those we meet during our busy day. That causes the fear and anger to grow. It even spreads to our lawmakers.

I know, you're saying that the lawmakers are the ones causing us to be angry and fearful. That's true. Just reverse the last paragraph. Their fear and anger trickle down to us. The news media helps spread these toxic emotions by continually repeating the same scary news and giving time and space to those who talk the loudest; i.e., those who are the most afraid and angry.

We know what the problem is. The question is how to reverse the situation. We can do that by each of us monitoring our emotions. When we feel afraid or angry, we can stop by recognizing that each of us (even people we don't like) is a perfect cosmos. Next, we do the right thing. We keep our focus on what needs to be done in our little corner of the world. We concentrate on those things for which we are grateful. Even in the worst of times, there are things to make us happy and jokes that make us laugh.

Just as fear and anger spread, so do gratitude and love. A wise woman once told me, "Peace, love, and joy is all there is."

I leave you with this question: Do you want to live in a world of peace, love and joy, or a world of anger and fear? Whatever we think and feel spreads, so make your choice and act upon it to the best of your ability.

Thank you, God, for sending us situations that encourage us to think and feel deeper than before. We see anger and fear and know that we can change it to more positive emotions. We've heard the saying, "Be the change you want to see." Open our hearts to believe that we have the power to change situations by changing our attitudes. Each open heart affects much more than we can imagine. We thank you for this opportunity to be a change agent leading the way to peace, love and joy!

CHOOSE PEACE

"One rageaholic can fill an entire office with anger, while a truly happy person can lighten the mood for everyone around her." - Martha Beck

We know the first part of the quote is true. We see it every day at work, on the news, in politics, and even in our neighborhoods and families. It is so easy to get caught up in another's emotions. That is why sports teams use cheerleaders and politicians use negative advertising.

Engaging in another person's anger or fear is detrimental to our own health and well-being. This is why wise teachers tell us to detach from the anger. Someone once said, "Anger is the face we put on fear." This is a good reminder to breathe deeply and let another's anger float past us instead of anchoring in our minds and hearts.

Let's be our own cheerleaders and fulfill the second part of the quote. Taking a deep breath (or several) will return us to our serenity and allow us to lighten the mood. Have you ever been in the midst of a confrontational discussion when someone interjects a joke? Did you notice how quickly the mood changed and your group was able to find a solution to whatever had everyone's undies in a bundle?

Just as anger and fear are contagious, so are calm and peace. Let's be our own cheerleaders and notice how quickly the mood around us softens and harsh words become gentle. How do we do that? Ms. Beck offered this lesson:

"You are never required to do more than you can do in peace. Right now, take a breath, return to peace, and refuse to leave."

Universe, thank you for your wisdom and guidance. Be with us this day, reminding us to come back to center if we begin to move into any extreme emotion. Remind us that we are much more powerful than we think. Remind us that our emotions can have far-reaching impact. Remind us that you never require us to do more than we can do in peace.

CHOOSE JOY

"Joy does not simply happen to us. We have to choose joy and keep choosing it every day." -Henri J. M. Nouwen

Many of us have come to believe that there are so much violence and natural disaster in our world that there is no room for joy. What is there to be joyful about? Storms, illness, traffic jams, angry bosses, sore backs and lack of money fill our reality. Why should we be joyful?

Joy doesn't have to be a 24/7 feeling. It can just be a moment:
when you look into a loved one's eyes;
when you see a flower bloom;
when you see your baby walk for the first time;
when your child graduates from college; or
when you feel the sun after days of rain.

Joy is momentary, but it can grow to be a habit, a way of life. We all have our ups and downs. Some of us are down more than up. That's okay. Life is not all grins and giggles. We face many situations that can and do suck joy from our lives.

If we want to experience joy on a regular basis, we can. The decision is ours. We can choose to feel joy every day, if only for a moment. Pamela Harper says, "How do you break this cycle? Allow yourself to be grateful for what is. You'll get used to joy." *

Spirit, we thank you for this day and choose to experience peace, love and joy. We know that perhaps we'll have to deal with a difficult situation, but we ask to see and feel joy where it exists.

* pamela@pamelaharper.com.

LET GO OF CONTROL

"Let go of what you can't control. Channel all that energy into living fully in the now." -Karen Salmansohn

So many of us spend way too many hours worrying about what might have been and what might be. There are very few things in life that we can control, so why worry about them?

Twelve Step programs have a saying, "Let go and let God." What has happened in the past remains in the past. Of course, if we have harmed someone, we must make amends or, at least, make an attempt. We cannot control what another person says or does. Our efforts may be received with forgiveness, or we may have lost a friend, or we may have the opportunity to learn what goes on behind those jail walls. Our reward comes from knowing that we attempted to make things right.

Another way to "Let go and let God" is in our daily lives. We have coworkers who rudely reject our friendship. We have no idea what has occurred in their past to make them shun us. All we can do is be polite when the occasion calls for it and let the rest go.

A big way of letting go and letting God is when we watch the news or hear stories about cruelty. We can write letters or send emails to change a politician or newsmaker's opinion, but we can't make them accept our vision of right actions. Disasters happen. We can send charitable donations, but we can't make the affected people use our gifts in the way that we feel is right. What these people do with our information and money becomes their decision.

The hardest place to "Let go and let God" is in our own homes. We see our loved ones acting rudely or destructively, but we can't stop their behaviors. If the person acting out is a child, we have an obligation to discipline and try new ways to help him or her live according to our beliefs. If that person is an adult, we have a responsibility to take precautions to assure that we and our children are safe and report their behavior to the authorities, if necessary. We can pray for their highest good. Beyond that, we are powerless. We can't stop another adult from acting in ways contrary to our beliefs.

17

"Let go of what you can't control. Channel all that energy into living fully in the now." We've been thinking about what we can and cannot control. Now it's time to move into living fully in the now. If we worry about the "mights," we have no energy to enjoy today. I once saw a poster that said, "Yesterday is gone. Tomorrow has not arrived. Today is a gift. That's why we call it the present." We need to accept where we are each moment, know that it is a gift, and be grateful, no matter what that moment contains.

Spirit, thank you for teaching us to live in the moment, the only time we have available. Yesterday is gone and tomorrow may or may not be. We choose to be grateful for each moment and to live it to the fullest. We choose to spend each moment living in peace, love and joy. We ask you to give everyone whatever is for that person's highest good.

TREAT YOURSELF

"Every day, give yourself at least three really good treats: One for every risk you take, and two because you're you. No exceptions. No excuses." Martha Beck*

Oh boy! I can have three desserts every day. I'm heading for the grocery store to buy something yummy. My waistline is grateful that Beck was probably not referring to desserts, though an occasional dessert is good for our souls too. Beck is referring to things that make our souls feel happy.

There are many ways we can treat ourselves. Treating ourselves regenerates our brains and bodies so that we can work more efficiently. Perhaps we could tell ourselves, "Way to go! You did a good job!" We could do a happy dance. (Hopefully, the boss isn't watching.) We could go for a walk and enjoy the sun warming our bodies. We could give ourselves a few minutes to play ONE game of Solitaire on our Kindles or work ONE crossword puzzle to get our minds off the project. Gratitude for ourselves also makes us aware of reasons to appreciate other people and the many wonderful ways in which they contribute to our happiness.

Regrettably, our society tends to consider treating ourselves as wasting time. Many of us were taught that to succeed we must "keep our noses to the grindstone." Perhaps we were told that good grades and hard work are the stepping stones on the path to success. They are, but we owe it to ourselves to take a break or two every day. Otherwise, we are not on the path to success; but, instead, on the road to a heart attack or mental collapse. Many employers offer their employees two 15-minute breaks and a lunch period. In the past, I either worked through those breaks and ate at my desk or spent the time complaining about the boss, coworkers and the work load. Spending free time like that can add to the level of anger floating around the world.

Fortunately, my current employer believes in another axiom, "All work and no play make Jack/Jill a dull boy/girl." For that reason, the employer schedules several team events throughout the year. These may be just for fun, to showcase a new event, or to support a good cause. These team events give employees time to relax and get to know their team-mates personally. It also reminds employees that their company appreciates their efforts toward making it a great place to work.

So take a few minutes to relax and show yourself some appreciation. You deserve it!

Spirit, thank you for this reminder to take a few moments several times a day to express gratitude for ourselves and our work. By being thankful for our own efforts, we are thanking you for giving us life, love and even things we don't like very much. This makes us better people.

*Beck, Martha, Daily Inspiration, info@marthabeck.com, February 3, 2016

CHOOSE CALM

"Hate is like acid. It can damage the vessel in which it is stored as well as destroy the object on which it is poured." -Ann Landers

Once again, our presidential election season is upon us. Is it just me, or does this campaign seem more vitriolic than usual? Every four years we as a nation go through this process, and each time accusations and insults fly like feathers at a chicken fight.

During the times when news traveled via weekly newspapers and letters that could take months to arrive, the writer usually took time to evaluate the consequences of his or her words before putting pen to precious, expensive paper. Some of their letters were quite pointed. Volatile arguments have continued throughout our history.

Perhaps one difference nowadays is that we have instant media and many more media outlets, so we are more aware of what the candidates and their supporters are saying. This allows those running for office, and the rest of us, to spout opinions without thinking about the potential damaging effects of this instant communication.

We may want to take a few minutes to examine our thoughts before sending them out to the world. Have we studied what we heard or thought we heard? Have we considered if there might be another aspect to that story? Have we considered how the words we send into the ether may affect the candidates or other voters?

Is this good for our individual well-being?

We are destroying the best part of ourselves and our nation by pouring the acid of hate upon those with whom we disagree. I must admit that I also participate in this destruction. I classify candidates by how I think they should act and occasionally make a statement to that effect. I can feel what these thoughts are doing to my internal self, and I know that others must be feeling the same. I'm concerned that many people are placing the blame for their irritation on the various candidates and are not focusing on the acid they pour on themselves.

Spirit, we ask that you guide us to evaluate our thoughts and words so we might not pour hate on anyone or anything, including ourselves. We know that guilt adds to the acid bath, so we ask you to show us how to be kind to ourselves as we become aware of our thoughts and actions while debating the issues.

* Warner, Carolyn, *Treasury of Women's Quotations*, Prentice Hall, 1992, page 40

FEARFUL OR PEACEFUL?

"Don't fight fearful thoughts. Just match each one with an alternative thought that brings you more peace." -Martha Beck

We all have fearful thoughts. What if I lose my job? Is that spot on my arm cancerous? If I die, what will happen to my family? What will I do if my loved one leaves? Those questions and so many more fill our waking hours and nag us in our dreams.

Martha Beck says to match each fearful thought with one that brings peace. That sounds too easy to be useful. Even so, let's think about what she says and see how it works by going through our questions one at a time.

What if I lose my job?

I have a job today and my family is fed. Deeply breathe. Relax your face, jaw, and neck muscles.

Is that spot on my arm cancerous?

I'll call the dermatologist for an appointment. She'll analyze it and offer a solution. Skin cancer is not fatal unless neglected, and I'm taking action. Deeply breathe. Relax your shoulders, arms and hands.

If I die, what will happen to my family?

The house is paid for and I have a good insurance policy. Take a deep breath. Relax your torso.

What if my loved one leaves?

I'll feel sad, but I won't die. Deeply breathe. Relax your lower extremities.

Now we are relaxed head to toe and can think clearly.

This seems like a rather simplistic look at life, but I know that it works. I've had, and still occasionally have, my brain and body in knots over both small and large events. However, once I decide to jump off the panic merry-go-round, take a few deep breaths, and look at my situation with open eyes, I see small actions I can take. By making one decision and then another, I soon find myself in a new and better situation.

Mike Dooley said the same thing with different words:
"When a thing hurts your eyes, stop looking at it.
When it hurts your ears, stop listening to it.
And when it hurts your heart, stop justifying it."

LAUGHTER HEALS ALL

"Laugh and be well." -Matthew Green

Years ago we often heard the saying, "Laughter is the best medicine." I think that quote came from Norman Cousins, the man who saved his life by concentrating on humor and happy thoughts. He was an example to all of us, even though we were too caught up in our worries to try it.

What can be more serious than saving your life? Nothing. But please let me tell my tale of healing through laughter.

Once, I was hit by some serious problems. Desperate for solutions, I tried Cousins' theory. For a year I focused on reading humorous books and watching comedies on television and at the movies. At first, the cure lasted only as long as the funny activity. I continued to fret and whine the rest of the time.

Eventually, the silliness began to sink into my soul. Problems became smaller and more manageable. At that point, I reduced my laughter cure to when I felt like the whole world was sitting on my shoulders. The next several years continued along those same lines, though I was able to see the humor in most situations.

About three years ago, I felt brave enough to join a humor writing group, and then another one. I soon learned that no matter how I felt when I turned on my computer, soon I would be laughing and feeling healthier. I also sought jobs that allowed me to have fun with my coworkers and guests.

Recently, I attended the National Society of Newspaper Columnists' annual conference in Hartford, Connecticut. Since the group did not have humor in its name and often the members' postings were about serious matters, I expected to have serious discussions. It turned out that many members of this group were also members of my humor groups. Even those who were not addressed their serious topics with humor. I laughed my way through three days of learning how to improve my writing skills.

As usual, I bought a stack of books in which the authors signed comments like, "Keep laughing," or "Don't stop laughing." When I arrived home, my problems were much lighter.

God would not have given us a sense of humor if we aren't supposed to use it. Joy is where we are meant to live.

Spirit, thank you for the gift of laughter. When we laugh we feel peace, love and joy. I can live a life of laughter because I know that is your precious gift and the path my life is meant to follow.

LIGHTEN UP

Often we take life much too seriously. We strive. We fear. We don't accomplish what we want to do. We even bring ourselves more problems.

That happened to me recently. Last month I made a big mistake on my checking account and had to pay a huge fee. That led me to worrying if I'd have enough money and to calling myself stupid. In return, I've had electronic equipment simply die, and I've experienced difficulties with other equipment. My energy level dropped.

Eventually, I remembered that I have nothing to fear. The Universe is taking care of me. I'm beginning to see those difficulties fading away. Energy is returning. Fun is returning. Joy is returning. Peace is returning.

Martha Beck, in the December, 2012, issue of "O" magazine says, "We need force only when we start from someplace other than peace, and serve purposes based on external judgments rather than internal joy... Remember how creation through play feels, because if [you] can remember this feeling, [you] can replicate it, and if [you] can replicate it, nothing can stop [you]."

How right she is! If we can relax and let life flow around us, we will see all our dreams come true. If we can take joy in the night sky, feel gifted when we admire beautiful spring flowers (despite the pollen on our cars), and see the wonders of God in a new baby's face, then we will know peace.

Back in the 1960's, many said, "Give peace a chance." At the same time, they were shouting, "Hell no, we won't go!" Buildings were bombed, whole neighborhoods were destroyed by riots, and our leaders were assassinated. All this happened because we were a country living in fear and anger.

If we can keep peace in our hearts, then words, events, conflicts and natural disasters will spur us to action without making us feel the weight of the world. Political dissention will float around us, but we know "this too shall pass." We may participate in these activities, but if we do it from peaceful hearts, we will make a difference.

27

Spirit, be with us this day. Show us your beauty and love. Remind us that inner peace will accomplish what striving cannot. Guide us as we learn what inner peace feels like and express that peace in our daily lives.

"Be not angry that you cannot make others as you wish them to be, since you cannot make yourself as you wish to be." -Thomas A' Kempis

Most of us try to change others. We've said, "My sweetie will change after we get married," or "My love will be a nicer person once the drinking stops." Marital status or sobriety doesn't change a person's basic self. Many of us have experienced or watched marriages go down the drain because one person expected the other to change after the wedding, and it didn't happen.

One of the first things we are told when we begin a twelve-step program, whether as a user or a family member, is, "If a person is a jerk when drunk, that person will be a jerk when sober." The jerk has to want to change. The same is true about whatever shortcomings we think the other person has. Changed behavior does not guarantee a nicer person.

The same statement is true of each of us. We want to change, but we don't. Or we change for a short time, only to fall into old habits. Why else do we make so many jokes about New Year's Resolutions? We know the resolutions are beginning to slide down the tubes at 12:01 a.m. on January 1.

If a person really wants to change, we will see miracles. We can change, but it's not easy. We need help and must be willing to accept that help, no matter where it comes from: prayer, challenge, or encouragement.

My mother used to tell this story about her smoking habit: She would cut back, often to just one cigarette a day, then something stressful would happen, and she would soon be back to a pack a day. It didn't matter if she prayed to stop, tried determination, asked someone to hide the cigarettes, or whatever else she thought might work.

At the same time, her pastor was fighting the battle of the scale. He prayed about his weight problem, went to weight-loss support groups, worked out at the Y. Nothing helped. He just couldn't get those extra pounds to come off. One day they were talking about their situations and made a vow. They would stop praying for themselves and pray for each other.

It wasn't long after that when my mother ran out of cigarettes during a blizzard. My dad offered to go to the store and get her some. She said, "No, I want to see if I can do without." She never smoked again. One of the last things she said before her transition was, "I haven't smoked for 40 years. I'm proud of that." Her pastor, well, he soon lost more than fifty pounds, seemingly effortlessly.

They were able to help each other but not themselves. Why is a mystery. The one thing we do know is that they truly wanted to change. Maybe just knowing that they each had someone in their corner facing the same issue was enough. I'm convinced that the answer is that they stopped focusing on their own bad behaviors and began focusing on the other person's good behaviors.

Spirit, we have been told that "the pot can't call the kettle black", but it never meant much. Now we see that it applies to each of us, no matter our situation. We have learned to stop praying, "God, help so-and-so to stop ____ behavior. Oh, I need help with that too." We now know to pray for the highest good of others, understanding that we do not know what their highest good is. We know to ask God to help us be the very best person we can be each day, whatever that is. Thank you for this awareness!

HEAL YOURSELF

"When our energy feels drained, we have allowed others to plug into us, without taking the time needed for ourselves, to recharge." - Window of Wisdom*

How often have we allowed others to drain our energy in order to please them? We were raised to be kind, thoughtful and caring by our parents, teachers and religious leaders. All of those are good traits. But in putting these into practice, we interpreted these teachings to mean give, give, give.

This is because we were not taught that, in order to give, we have to take care of ourselves first, usually because our role models did not know how to take care of themselves. I remember watching my mother and aunts work until they were ready to drop, taking care of everyone in the family. Our fathers and uncles worked their jobs and farms, came home, made repairs, and then went to a neighbor's house to do what needed to be done there.

They did this day after day. Taking a break to rest or relax was considered selfish. No matter how bad life was for them, someone else had it worse and needed their help. They became exhausted because they were not nurturing themselves. As the years passed, we saw their bodies fail from overwork.

As our generation grew to adulthood, some of us followed our parents' model of giving. Others became takers. As the years passed, most of us learned that there is a middle way that is healthier for all. We have learned that we must not only give to others, but we must also take time for ourselves. Only in this way can we keep the energy flowing in both directions.

It doesn't matter how we take care of ourselves. Perhaps we dance or practice yoga, bike or garden, or read until our eyes close and we slip into a restful nap. I do all of the above, different methods for different days.

The point is that by taking time to heal myself mentally, physically and spiritually, I have more energy to give to others. I pushed myself to the limit while raising my children, much to their detriment and my regret. During the years between their leaving home and my introduction to my grandchildren, I learned a new way: to take care of myself first.

Now I work, spend time with my great-grandsons, read, meditate, spend time enjoying the outdoors, and write. I'm not all the way there, because I find writing healing and restful, but it seems to be lowest on my list of things to do for myself.

* Window 742 – "Don't diminish your light," April 15, 2015
https://awindowofwisdom.wordpress.com

GROWING

"During the times we think we're being unproductive, the seeds of new worlds are germinating within us, and they need peace to grow." -Martha Beck

Most of us don't buy into Beck's philosophy. We've been taught from childhood that we must be busy every moment. Nothing will get done if we lie down to read or nap. The sky will fall if we don't wash the dishes as soon as everyone finishes eating. We actually begin to clear the table while the slower eaters are still savoring their meals.

People like Leonardo DaVinci, Isaac Newton and Thomas Edison were held up as role models, as they should. These men were prodigious producers that changed, and are still changing, our world with their inventions. Nobody bothers to consider whether they ever took a day off from their discoveries. Don't you think that they might have sat outside watching people and letting their thoughts wander?

DaVinci saw a world of beauty and scientific possibilities even in a time of poverty and rudimentary tools. He was born with the talent, but the otherworldly beauty and future practicality of his work had to come from his genius imagining distant possibilities.

We're taught that the only person who took a nap productive was Isaac Newton. He, supposedly, was napping under a tree when an apple fell on his head. This fortuitous event demonstrated that gravity existed. Don't you think he'd been considering gravity for years? We all see things fall from the time that we throw our teddy bears out of the crib. Being more aware than most of us, Newton began forming ideas about what made things fall. The apple hitting his head just made his ideas gel into the theory of gravity.

We're not all DaVincis, Newtons or Edisons, but we all have the ideas we need inside us. We can't hear those ideas if we are constantly tuned in to the noise around us. We can't see the ideas if we're constantly worrying about cutting the grass before it rains. Very often, we get our best ideas when we're quiet, our minds empty, enjoying the sunlight streaming through the trees, listening to the waves hit the beach, or watching the nightly star shows.

Spirit, thank you for placing all the knowledge we need within our minds and bodies. We ask that today you make us aware that the knowledge is there. We open ourselves to listen, to see and know that all will be made obvious when the time is right. When we need to help a friend, the impulse will be there. When we need to fix a leaky faucet, the knowledge will be there. Thank you for showing us that we're not just on this Earth to bumble and fumble. We are here to live in peace, love and joy – and producing. We just need to stop, listen, and understand our instructions.

LET GO OF RESULTS

"The answer to every question beginning with 'Why' begins with 'Because I love you.' Actually I love you anyway —and the answer to every question beginning with 'How' begins with 'None of your beeswax.'" TUT – A Note from the Universe

We can find all sorts of advice telling us how to get the things we want: true love, a new house, a better job, a lottery prize, and so on. We can make extensive lists of our desires. Advisors tell us to think positively, make a vision board, meditate on the desire, light a candle, or chant to focus our attention. What they don't tell us is the why and the how.

Why is my mother's health failing? Why haven't I won the lottery yet? (I don't buy any tickets!). Why am I stuck in this job? Why hasn't my true love appeared?

The Universe says, "Because I love you." Our vision is only limited by our comprehension. We don't know what lessons we need to learn first. Perhaps we need to feel pain before we can fully appreciate joy. Maybe our mother is ill so that we can learn compassion. Maybe our love has not appeared because we want someone to rescue us rather than being a true partner. Sometimes the Universe lets us know right away what the lesson is. At other times, events are puzzles until one day the light comes on within us, and we see the lessons and the results.

How we get the things we want or need is a bit trickier, because. the Universe tells us, "None of your beeswax." We can make the vision board if we wish. We can burn a candle and chant. The gift cannot arrive unless we are completely clear about what we want and willing to leave the details up to the Universe. If we change details, the Universe has to start the search all over again.

For example, we may want a job that pays more than our current one and also nourishes our soul as we help others. So we tell the Universe that we want to work for ABC Company in a particular position. Then, a few months down the road, we may decide we'd rather work for XYZ Company. So the Universe has to begin again.

35

To get the perfect job we need to stick to our initial statement – a job that pays more, feeds our soul and helps others.

Next comes the hard part—letting go of the details so the Universe can work on our behalf. This requires sitting in our truth and trusting the Universe as our life unfolds. It may turn out that our perfect job is with LMNOP Company. It feeds our soul, allows us to help others, and pays twice what we wanted!

My best example is my house. When I moved to Williamsburg, I lived in low-income housing and was not happy. I had just found my meditation group, and someone there suggested that I manifest my own house. Impossible! But, I gave it a try. I wanted a quiet neighborhood with residents of varying ages and races. I wanted trees. I wanted a lot of windows. I wanted this and that feature. Then, thinking it would never happen, I let go of the details.

Soon someone told me about a low-income home buyers' program operated by my county. I visited my caseworker and gave her the information that she requested. Then I took the required classes. Eventually, the caseworker called and said, "You are qualified to buy a house valued at a certain price." I contacted my daughter's real estate agent and then faced several delays before she found three houses that fit my requirements. On the big day, my daughters and I appeared at her office, only to learn that two of the houses were off the market. We decided to look at the one remaining house.

My daughters walked through the door first, turned to me (still on the porch) and said, "This is your house, Mom." After looking around, I agreed. I bid what the agent suggested. The owner accepted my bid even though other people had bid more. The paper work wound its way through the bureaucracy, and soon I was moving into MY house. All this happened within a year.

Universe, I say that I trust you to provide for my highest good, but I often tell you how to accomplish that. I withdraw all my instructions. As of this moment, I trust you to handle the why, how and when, because this is what you have promised us. I ask only for that which is for my highest good.

36

ENJOY THE SILENCE

"In every walk with nature one receives far more than he seeks."
-John Muir

Even though we just had a snow storm and temperatures are in the basement, this quote still fits today. Most of us are not out walking with nature today because of the cold, but we can gaze out the window and absorb the beauty and silence. While looking out the window, we can sip a cup of hot cocoa and notice that the world's tempo seems to have slowed.

If you have to shovel out your car and drive slippery streets to your job (grumble), you can still take in the beauty. You have to prepare - boots, gloves and hats (grumble, grumble). Take your time shoveling so you don't have a heart attack (grumble, grumble, grumble). Each time you stop to gather your energy, you can admire the frosty air coming from your mouth and nose. You can enjoy the intriguing shadows that bare trees make on the snow and the green of the holly bushes. You may be lucky enough to see a flash of red as a cardinal lands on your bird feeder.

While looking around at the snowy landscape, we can let our minds wander through the year. In April we see the glorious azalea blooms. Later on, irises stun our senses with their many colors. Pretty soon we see bright yellow blossoms and tiny green tomatoes in our garden. Each season has its own glory and its own purpose. One of those purposes is preparing us for days like this, when we can look out the window or take a walk in the woods. We have no work to do today except to enjoy the beauty of this restful season.

If we can enjoy that mindset – even for just a minute – we receive more than we seek. Our jobs are important, but our ability to be silent for a moment to take it all into our souls is more important.

Creator, we thank you for our beautiful world and our ability to absorb that beauty. We know that you have given us this day to enjoy and the clothes to dress warmly. We send out caring thoughts, asking you to take care of those who are struggling to survive. We know that you gave us this day to reflect and the choice to enjoy or to complain. We choose to receive the day as a gift, no matter how we use the time.

RACING THOUGHTS

"Agnes: It feels like my thoughts are racing in tiny Formula One cars, up one side of my brain and down the other. Some crash and burn, some stall and hit the wall, some blow a motor and leave a toxic trail of antifreeze and busted parts. It just makes me crazy. How do you keep your thoughts from driving you crazy?"

Trout: "I don't buy 'em cars."

From "Agnes" cartoon, August 1, 2014 -Tony Cochran

Many of us experience life like Agnes does. Our thoughts race through our brains like Formula One cars: crashing, stalling or blowing motors. Those thoughts clutter the track and don't allow thoughts that are still operating to drive through the mess and get to the finish line. Then, like Agnes, we feel like we're going crazy. We can't make good decisions because of all the debris.

Often we can't sleep because of all the cars roaring around inside our brains. We don't give proper attention to the task at hand, be it driving, developing a business plan, or playing with children. We miss what is important.

We don't see the car that just cut off the driver ahead of us, and we miss taking proper precautions to avoid an accident.

We type incorrect numbers into our business plan that would have given us the information we need to succeed.

We miss that precious moment when our child reveals what is on his/her mind. We only hear the words and not the meaning behind them. "I'm afraid of spiders," could mean "I'm afraid of my teacher."

So what do we do about it? Like Trout, we "don't buy 'em cars." We have to deliberately slow our thoughts to walking speed. Only in that way can we discern whether this thought or that one will help us and those around us. I know, easier said than done. However, once we learn how to slow our thoughts, life will begin to bloom around us.

Several years ago I arrived at a meeting and announced, "I saw flowers today. I heard the birds singing." I had not realized how

39

much of life was absent because I had given all my attention to my racing thoughts.

We have many ways to learn to slow our thoughts. We can notice that our breathing is fast and shallow and take a moment to breathe deeply and slowly. After practicing a while, we'll notice when our breathing is too rapid and automatically slip into conscious breathing.

We can meditate. We can do formal practices like yoga or meditation while focusing on a candle flame (always good for our mental and physical health). Prayer is good, if done consciously. Babbling our mixed-up thoughts to our Creator just keeps the wheels turning. Sitting down and allowing our thoughts to float away helps. A walk in the woods is refreshing. When exercising, we tend to start our routine with rapid, incomplete repetitions, but soon we slow into a deliberate pattern that helps both our body and mind. These are just a few observations and suggestions. If we stop for a minute and think about what works, we'll realize our best choices.

All of these methods and many more have the same result. They slow our breathing and our thoughts. We can focus on the issue at hand and make conscious decisions based on our needs and wants, not just what seems easiest at the time or which race car is damaged least. We clear our thought tracks of debris. We can stride to the finish line carrying the checkered flag.

Creator Spirit, thank you for teaching us to slow down to get more done. Thank you for giving us methods to slow those race cars in our brain. Thank you for giving us clear thought patterns. You made us with brains and bodies that help us reach our goals. This is a gift we treasure and use with care.

SOLUTION TO VIOLENCE

"Forgiving is the only real solution to violence." -Nancy H. Glende

Looking at all the violence in our world, we can feel that those words sound like an insurmountable goal. Too many of us have experienced violence. "Forgive" was a word that always gave me problems. However, three wise people explained what it actually meant, giving me a new perspective.

The first was a priest who said, "To forgive doesn't mean that justice isn't done." He explained that if an incident requires legal action, we call the police and follow through by testifying in court. If the action is more personal, such as harsh words, we can sever our relationship with that toxic person. This is not always possible, especially if the injury occurs within our family. Even so, the priest said that we need to take what steps we can to protect ourselves in the future. He also explained that revenge is not justice.

The second person was Dr. Phil McGraw on an Oprah show. He was talking to a woman whose carelessness had led to her child's death. Dr. Phil said, "Do you think your child is sitting in heaven hating you? Do you think he wants you to continue living with the guilt?" Hearing that, I sat down at my computer and emailed my three adult children telling them that I was going to let go of the guilt of being a poor mother. They each responded, "It's about time, and you weren't as bad as you think you were."

The third person was a friend who said, "To me, forgiving means letting go of the pain." Ah, finally a concept I can understand! I can let go of anger, resentments, and disappointments.

I think that was the day I began to heal on a deeper level.

Eventually, it dawned on me that since I had changed, the people who hurt me had probably changed too. You know what? They have. None of us is the same person we were 10, 20, or 40 years ago when the hurt happened.

Somewhere in this process I realized that the hurt didn't run just one way. I had caused pain too and had to let go of my guilt, not just as a parent, but also as a wife, daughter, coworker, and friend. It was easy to say, but not so easy to do. Even so, we can do it by being kinder to ourselves.

Have you noticed that I haven't mentioned the people who have caused monumental pain and death? That is because each of them began with a minor pain or resentment that they allowed to let grow until they punished those who were perceived as enemies. None of us is immune from horrific acts. We like to think we are, but if we look back on our actions, we can see how they could have grown into violence under different circumstances.

Spirit, thank you for teaching us that we can let go of pain and resentment. We do not need to carry this heavy weight around. We learn day by day that we can only live in peace, love and joy when we let go of hurts. This you have promised us. And so it is.

THINK PEACE

"Make your mind part of the world's peace, instead of its fear, and I promise, life will get better and better." -Martha Beck*

We're still wading through the winter holidays that continue through New Year's Day. We try to focus on a season of peace and goodwill, but often we get sidetracked and hit by the "winter blahs." At home we may experience family dissention as we stand in the kitchen washing mounds of dishes, growling to ourselves, "This is the season of joy, dammit!" We may experience lack – of everything. Or we may be lucky enough to share our bounty with a family who cares.

Then, as the holidays wind to an end, we stop celebrating long enough to watch the news and remember all the hate and violence that is occurring in our neighborhoods and around the world. We sigh and wonder if that can be changed or if we are doomed to live this way forever.

I can say without doubt – NO! Just as Martha Beck says, if we set our minds on peace and act on that each day, our world will get better. I can hear you all saying, "Yeah, right." However, it's true. When we think peace and kindness, we act out our beliefs, often not even aware that we are doing it. Each act will affect another person.

Remember the old shampoo commercial. If you tell two people and they tell two people, soon everyone will use this product due to word of mouth. Just as telling others about shampoo will convince them to buy it, our actions will eventually create peace. World peace probably will not happen anytime soon, but at least we can make our own little corner of the world a friendlier place.

I can see you shaking your head in doubt. "You don't know the jerks I have to deal with." I, too, felt that way for many years. Then I became tired of feeling anger and stress. I determined that I would create calm for myself. Now each day when I get up, I state firmly, "I choose to be the best person I can be today." As time passes, I find that making that choice makes my actions become kinder. As a result, I notice that people are kinder to me. All this makes family life, friendships and the work place kinder. I *want* to be with those people, instead of feeling obligated to be with them.

Spirit, thank you for this beautiful day. Even if it's raining or snowing, the day is still beautiful. Thank you for knowing that if we become calm, life around us will become calm. Life can be wonderful if we believe it to be so. We choose to act on that belief, knowing that all is happening for our highest good.

* "Daily Inspiration," Martha Beck, December 25, 2015
info@marthabeck.com

ANGRY LIVES

"Life appears to me too short to be spent in nursing animosity or registering wrong." – Charlotte Bronte

"You cannot shake hands with a clenched fist." – Indira Gandhi

"What I've learned about being angry with people is that it generally hurts you more than it hurts them." – Oprah Winfrey

People seem to be angry lately. We were angry in the '60s and '70s, but we seemed to come back to our senses and live more quietly. During the decades since, our world made a lot of strides and a lot of mistakes, but we grew and lived together in relative peace; that is, until the past few years when our personal, national and international anger have grown and become more dangerous for the citizens of many countries, including our own.

In some countries the citizens are overthrowing their governments. Others are being invaded by larger and better-armed neighbors. Some people think that anyone who has a different outlook on life should be killed. In our own country, more and more people who feel alienated decide to take it out on others; sometimes on many others. We then grieve for those who gave their lives.

Some of our politicians seem to think that the only way to achieve their ends is to set up blocks to any kind of progress or change. Some seem to think that anything proposed by the other political party is evil and must be obliterated. Some seem to think that particular politicians are determined to destroy our country. This was the attitude in the years leading up to and including the Civil War and several years after.

Do we want to relive those years with more deadly weapons?
Are we willing to see that we all bleed the same color of blood?
Are we willing to try to accept our neighbors for who they are?
Are we and our politicians willing to listen to others' opinions?
Are we willing to accept that we all want the same outcome but are approaching the problem from different angles?

Are we willing to talk to each other and learn what is in the other person's heart?

Or are we going to continue to act on what we think the other person is thinking?

Creator, thank you for this beautiful world and all the people and creatures on it. Open our eyes to see that all of us just want what we think is best for our loved ones. Open our hearts so each of us can learn to accept the other for who he or she is inside. Open our minds to be willing to reach out to those we think are our enemies. I ask this for each person on our planet Earth, no matter who he or she may be.

TRUST THAT ALL IS AS IT SHOULD BE

"Keep going. Everything you need will come to you at the perfect time." Pamela Harper*

Harper went on to say, "When you trust your Creator, your Creator trusts you. To attract health, wealth or happiness you must first believe that all things in Divine order are possible for you. As you set intentions with faith, you expect that they'll arrive on time just as you visualize them or as you anticipate another tomorrow. Believe, trust and act as if you are the Co-Creator you are meant to be."

Often we worry about so many things in our lives: family, health, wealth, friends, transportation, jobs, education…This list could go on for pages. We love to worry. We tend to make worry our main occupation. When we meet someone who doesn't worry, we wonder what's wrong with them. How did they get so lucky that everything is wonderful in their world?

We feel justified about our worry when bad things happen. A loved one crosses to the other side. We lose a job. We don't get a scholarship to the college of our choice. Then we get sick, heart-sick, depressed, and often give up on our dreams. When we give up, anger becomes the dominant force in our lives.

I know this is true, because I've been there. I've thought that my life was destined to be one of disappointments, that I would never reach my dreams. When I finally reached the point that I said, "If this is all there is, then this is all there is," a new attitude began creeping into my awareness. I began to say thank you for everything—a filling breakfast, a safe trip to work, the kindness of my co-worker. Of course, most of all I was grateful that my family was near and that they seemed to actually like me. I have found that the more I noticed and appreciated, the more that good things came my way – a new generation to love, nicer friends, a better job….

Sun, rain, and snow all come in the proper season. Currently, in my part of the U.S., we're wondering when they are going to balance themselves. Our days are hot and humid, causing us to wilt when we

47

want to be playing outside. Then a sudden rainstorm hits and barely cools the temperature while raising the humidity. We feel like we're living in a greenhouse, and it's miserable. But greenhouses are where flowers develop their most beautiful blooms. I'm hoping that I'll bloom too.

This is not to say that all is fantastic in my world. I still tend to worry about this and that. But I remember that "Everything you need will come to you at the perfect time," and I relax and let life flow over me as it will. When I live according to that philosophy, life is easier, and the things I need do come to me.

Spirit, thank you for this gift of knowing that all is in Divine order, and that all will come in the proper time

*Inspiration, July 13, 2015, "Mutual Trust"
Pamela@pamelaharper.com

OVERCOMING ANGER

"With rage in heart and clenched fists, you may feel invincible. The truth is that you have never been weaker." -Dr. Phil McGraw[1]

Life has a way of bringing our situations full-circle. We face who we used to be and learn who we are now. This last week circumstances made me proud of whom I've become.

Many years ago, I married a nice young man who said he loved me. I thought he was fun to be with, so I convinced myself that I loved him. I thought he would rescue me from my parents who set many rules and made my life miserable. After our wedding, we immediately moved across the U.S. to his military posting. We had some fun and some arguments.

After three children and several military assignments, we found that life was not so much fun and that the arguments were nearly non-stop. (Of course, none of this was my fault.) We parted ways, both carrying a great deal of anger and feeling fully justified in our actions. As often happens with divorced couples, our communications were rancorous and filled with threats. Eventually the children finished high school, and we no longer needed to communicate. This gave us a good, long cooling off time. I could feel my anger lessen as time went by, and I began to admit my contributions to the discord.

Our first visit eight years ago was touchy, but amicable. We were determined to put the past behind us. His wife and I became fast friends, and I wondered where the man I had hated so many years had gone. Then he asked for directions to another relative's city. Our daughters explained several times that he would need to go west several miles, then turn north to get there. No matter how many times they explained, he insisted, "I don't want to go west and north. I want to go northwest." I chuckled and said to myself. "Oh, he's still in there." As the years have passed, we've met a few more times with cautious conversation. Our extended family has blended well.

Last weekend was the BIG event. His family always gathers for a reunion the first Sunday in July. I've been invited several times by various relatives, but I have always turned them down for fear I'd be considered an interloper or even be excoriated for my behavior. This year I decided it was time to face the crowd. I knew I had changed and thought I could handle the situation, whatever it turned out to be.

One daughter and family drove to the mountains in one vehicle. I rode with the other daughter and husband. It was not an auspicious beginning. Traffic jams and motion sickness reigned supreme. I spent a good part of the trip holding onto the headrest in front of me to keep from swaying and staring at it to avoid catching any movement out of the side of my eyes. Along the way I bought Dramamine, but I still maintained the same position, feeling only slightly stable, until we reached our destination.

Of course, everyone there thought this was hilarious, but they sympathized while trying to keep straight faces. As my agony dispersed, I began to interact with those present and found that I was having fun. The entire visit turned out to be much better than I expected. I didn't keep myself sheltered emotionally, but instead let events happen as they would. Even frequent rainstorms did not dampen our spirits. We laughed at the children playing in the mud, and we cooked for many visitors. We enjoyed seeing old friends and relatives at the reunion until the rain washed out the event, and we all ran for our cars.

I felt like I belonged with these wonderful people. Even the "ex" and I enjoyed a few laughs and the "remember-whens." I knew then that we both had finally grown into the people we were supposed to be all those years ago, before anger led us astray.

Oh, the trip back was much better. I took Dramamine before we left the hotel and followed family advice about resting my head against a stationary surface and keeping my eyes closed until we were out of the mountains. I'm looking forward to seeing them again – down here in the flat lands.

My conclusion was confirmed the next day at work. A man I'd never met before said, "I sense you are a calm person. You don't have anger in you." I didn't know how to respond, but WOW! What a wonderful gift from a stranger!

Spirit, thank you for this gift of serenity after all those years of anger!

[1]"O, the Oprah Magazine", January 2015, pg. 41

LET GO OF ANGER

"When angry, count four; when very angry, swear." -Mark Twain (Samuel Clemens) *

Recently I wrote a piece in which I described no longer feeling anger at a person who had wronged me. A friend challenged that statement, so today I am attempting to provide a fuller explanation of my thoughts.

Anger is a normal part of the human psyche. We all feel anger. We get angry at our family, jobs, the world situation, and human behavior in general. There are so many things in this world that can trigger our anger button. Feeling anger is sometimes appropriate. It's how we act on that anger that is right or wrong.

Do we shout and swear? Do we vow to get even? Do we stop speaking to that person? Do we refuse to see that person ever again? Do we carry our anger forever? I've seen all those reactions and have done some of them. The results are always destructive rather than constructive.

Or we can focus our anger another way. If someone makes us angry, we can walk away and consider what triggered our anger. Was it really what they did? Was it a reflection of an old memory? Should we go back and apologize for our behavior? Should we just let the anger fly away in the wind?

Perhaps if our anger is at a larger situation, we can become an active part of the solution. Are we angry that too many children can't read? Then we can we become a reading tutor. Are we angry at a social situation? Perhaps we can take a page from Mahatma Mohandas Gandhi and lead a march to the sea, or we can emulate one of his followers, Dr. Martin Luther King, and organize voter registration (still an issue these many years later).

I often get angry about my physical well-being. I'm not as strong as I'd like to be. I can't do what I did when I was 18. I'm not really sick, but various restrictions and prescriptions make me angry. I'm learning a different tactic for this situation: Acceptance.

I can accept that the other person is not who I'd like him or her to be and move forward accordingly. I can accept that the world situation is not what I'd like to see, and, if I'm so moved, I can do as the bumper stickers say: "Think globally. Act locally," or "Imagine Whirled Peas."

For many things in my life, I live acceptance. However, yesterday my doctor told me to take yet another nutritional supplement to temporarily forego donating blood (something that means a lot to me) and to have yet another yucky test. I became angry. I didn't accept her diagnosis and became what she called "cranky." As the day passed, I realized that she was just looking out for my health. She didn't tell me that I had a horrible disease. She just told me to adjust my life a little for my ultimate good. I'm still not happy about taking yet another pill, but I'm glad it's a supplement and not a medicine.

A friend recently told me how she recovered from a serious illness. She was following all her doctor's directions, but feeling angry that she was in so much pain. Finally, she reached a point where she said, "Okay, God, if this is to be my life, I accept it. Just show me where to go from here." Amazingly, from that point she began to heal a little at a time. She can now participate in activities that were once unthinkable. She's not playing tennis yet, but she can do pretty much what she wants to do otherwise; i.e., work, socialize and just feel good.

"God, grant me the serenity to accept the things I cannot change, courage to change the things I can, and the wisdom to know the difference." **

*Pg. 89, *Pudd'nhead Wilson*, Chapter X, "Pudd'nhead Wilson's Calendar"
**The Serenity Prayer, A Day at a Time in Al-Anon, 1987, Al-Anon Family Groups

WORRY IS A BURDEN

"Worry does not empty tomorrow of its sorrow. It empties today of its strength." -Corrie ten Boom

We all worry. Some of us just worry a little. Some people make a career of fretting and showing their love by worrying. They think a non-worrier doesn't care what happens to the people they love.

It's natural to be concerned about outcomes, but spending valuable time worrying rather than taking steps to correct the situation is futile. A friend once said, "Worry is like a rocking chair. It doesn't get you anywhere, but it gives you something to do while you wait."

Having grown up in a household where worry was a valuable commodity, I was shocked when my mother-in-law had one son in Vietnam, one in Thailand and one in the Mediterranean all at the same time and seemed very relaxed about their safety. I asked why she wasn't worried. She responded, "They are all at least ten thousand miles from here. If something happens, there is nothing I can do to help the situation. All I can do is trust God to take care of them." I wasn't sure about that until many years later when all three of my children were on active duty at the same time. Remembering what she said gave me daily comfort.

Recently I was concerned that I was nowhere near reaching a goal I had set for myself. My daily process was to beat up on myself mentally, working up a good-sized-worry stew. Knowing this was futile, but unable to stop, I talked to a friend who said, "Remember that what is to be comes easily and effortlessly. If you have to struggle, then your goal is not right for you." Just hearing that stopped the worry and freed me to take steps to change the goal to something I could reach.

God, we are grateful that all situations will result in outcomes that are for our highest good. We know that worry is futile and will only disrupt the unfolding of our future. Relaxing, trusting and knowing that whatever is happening will be better with the morning sun. Thank you for this promise!

Chapter Three: Challenge Yourself

LETTING GO

"Let it go. Let it out. Let it all unravel. Let it free, and it can be a path on which to travel." -Unknown*

Often we deal with hurts by burying them and stewing for the rest of our lives. That means we feel our feelings in a self-destructive manner. The quote suggests that we "Let it go. Let it out."

Some people think that letting it out means that we scream and yell at the person who hurt, insulted or challenged us. While there are a few occasions that method will work, most times emotional outbursts will make it worse. We can try to discuss the situation quietly and see what happens. If that doesn't resolve the situation, we have other options for letting it out.

We can journal, talk to a friend, talk with a professional, and feel the feelings until they dissipate. Most situations that upset us to that extent need a combination of those options. We can journal and talk to a trusted friend. If that doesn't work, we may seek professional help. Along the way we need to feel the fear, pain, anger, sadness, abandonment, disappointment or other label that will name the problem.

Actually, naming what we're feeling is the hardest part. We often tell people that we are disappointed or concerned to be diplomatic. Those are appropriate labels when you confront someone or are talking to a supervisor. When you are naming your feelings either to yourself or to an appropriate third party, you can, and probably should, use stronger language. You can say whatever you need to say to get the feelings out.

Once the feelings are out in the open, you can begin letting go. In Al-Anon and AA, one of the most used phrases is "Let go and let God," meaning that we must let go our stranglehold on the problem before God can take it away. Another common phrase is "Anything an Al-Anon member lets go of has claw marks all over it," meaning that we hold on until the pain simply slips off the ends of our fingers from its weight.

Do you want to go through life holding on until the pain eventually slides out of your grip? Or would you rather let go before the weight gets too heavy and your healing can begin before the wounds destroy your body and your mind? Would you prefer to walk a smoother path, as the quote says?

My choice, after carrying hurt for many years, was to begin letting it go. What a gift that was! Life is so much easier and lighter, the path smoother without the weight of old pains. That's not to say I'm perfectly adjusted now, just much better and getting better yet.

Spirit, thank you for teaching us that we don't have to carry the weight of old and new pains. We can release ourselves from this burden by letting it go. We know that you will transmute the pain to feelings of calm. We know and trust that this is so for each of us.

*Unknown author, quoted on December 22, 2015 post at pamela@pamelaharper.com, "Inspiration 12-23-15: 'Loving all of you'"

STEPS TO HEALING

"When you heal yourself on the inside, everything else around you no longer triggers old pain." A Window of Wisdom*

Releasing old pain allows us to experience a lighter, happier life. We cause ourselves harm by concealing our pain. We need to release our negative feelings. Today let's think about ways to heal ourselves on the inside.

The idea that has been floating around mental therapists and religious teachers for many years is forgiveness. An old saying tells us to "forgive and forget." It's easy to say I forgive this person for doing that to me or my loved one. But do we actually forgive? Forgiving means to release the pain. That's a tough job. From my own experience I'll say that it's almost impossible to forget. We may forget what $E=MC^2$ means but we seldom, if ever, forget an insult or other situation that causes us pain.

Recently a friend told me about a better way to release old pain. That is to thank the person for the role he or she played in your life because it affected who you are today. That may not be possible or safe to pursue. An easier and safer way may be to write that person a letter pouring out your feelings while acknowledging the way that person's actions made you a better person. How is that possible? Perhaps a person telling you repeatedly that you were stupid made you determined to prove them wrong. Maybe it encouraged you to pursue higher education or get a job requiring excellent mental skills.

I can hear you saying, "I wouldn't dare send a letter thanking so and so for what he or she did. That would put me in danger, or, at minimum, it would bring their ire raining down on me." Only mail the letter if you feel 100% safe. You don't have to mail the letter. Just writing out the facts and feelings releases the old "stuff." You can burn the letter and allow the pain to float to the clouds with the smoke. You can tear the letter to bits and send it to the landfill with the rest of your trash or release it to a river to float out to the sea.

A quicker method my friend suggested is to picture the offending person in your mind and mentally or verbally thank them for making you the person you have become. Either method is incredibly freeing. If you do this, choosing to be free of the old pain, you will be.

Spirit, thank you for teaching us that we don't have to carry the weight of old and new pains. We can release ourselves from this burden by thanking the offender for the role they played in our lives. We know that you will transmute the pain to feelings of freedom. We know and trust that this is so for each of us, no matter our situation.

*A Window of Wisdom 1007, January 6, 2016

TAKE STEPS

"…Many are waiting for their life to take off. Who's going to tell them that this could be their problem? Don't wait, do something, anything, everything you can think of." -The Universe*

How many years have we wasted waiting for life to take off, for success to arrive, or for a gigantic pay raise?

Well, we can all agree that's not going to happen unless we put some effort behind the wait. We hear so many stories about people achieving instant success as overnight sensations. We don't hear that the musician played for years at local bars for what beer he could drink during his show. We don't hear that the famous artist waited tables while earning an MFA degree. We don't hear about the writer who has fourteen unsold novels and one hundred rejection letters in her closet.

I must admit that I am one of those who quit when the going got hard. My parents believed that success belonged to the wealthy and that poor people worked until they died, still poor. But I can't blame my parents. I had more opportunities than they, yet I still always hoped that prosperity would come from the end of a fairy's wand. Of course, life didn't turn out that way. I had some successes and some failures and overall have earned a place a little higher on the prosperity ladder than my parents enjoyed.

Still, I always wanted to say, "I did this," or, "I was presented that award." It may be that one day I'll be able to say those things, but I've finally learned that, as much as I don't want to, I need to work for what I want. It took me long enough to face that fact. One role model who inspires me is Thomas Edison, inventor of the electric light bulb, the phonograph and many other useful items. He said, "Opportunity is missed by most people because it is dressed in overalls and looks like work."

Work is what I always tried to avoid. So, here I am, just now learning about being willing to work. Sometimes it's still hard. I get up in the morning and want to read the paper and reply to emails while I relax in my recliner. Then I choose to go for a walk or solve a puzzle, but not work. It's not easy to break a life-long habit of waiting for success to fall in my lap.

But, here I am putting these words on paper. This means I have started taking steps to reach my goals.

Spirit, thank you for this awareness, even though it has come late in life. If I'm willing to put in the effort, I know that all will turn out for my highest good. Just as we must make an effort to be kind and caring, we must also make an effort to earn our successes.

*Mike Dooley, TUT – A Note from the Universe, April 25, 2016, theuniverse@tut.com

MOVE FORWARD

"He that will not sail until all dangers are over, will never put to sea." -Thomas Fuller

Often, fear rules our lives. We are bombarded with messages telling us to be afraid: jobs are hard to find, people are killing people, medicine has dangerous side effects and much more.

Living in fear is easier than facing the world. Or is it? If we're afraid of crowds, we may miss a Memorial Day parade with all the smiling children, marching bands and veterans to whom we owe our freedom. Even more, we'll miss lunging for the candy being tossed from floats.

If we're afraid that we can't find a better work situation, we may spend years being miserable in a job that doesn't fit our skills. We may stay in a loveless marriage because we fear not being able to support our children.

Being afraid can shield us from danger, but it can also deprive us of joy, love and laughter. So how do we release these fears and live in the moment?

The answer is easy, but applying it is not. Twelve-Step programs have a saying, "Let go and let God," just five short words that sound do-able, but applying them feels like we're about to climb Mount Everest wearing a bikini and carrying a walking stick.

To let go of fear, we must trust that we have the skills, knowledge and courage to move ahead. Trust is another tricky word. It's only five letters long but packed with years of old lessons, often learned the hard way.

How long will it take us to brave the outside world? That depends on our determination to let go of what no longer serves us. We must realize that we won't exhibit bravery until we let go of what is holding us back. Most often our steps are small. The size of the steps is not important, consistency is. Daily practice will let us "put to sea."

Spirit, we ask you to guide us as we take tiny steps to a better life. We trust that You and your angels will be with us each moment, holding our hands and whispering encouraging thoughts in our ears. We let go of this prayer with gratitude, knowing that it is so.

TRY AGAIN

"Sometimes courage is the quiet voice at the end of the day saying, I will try again tomorrow." -Mary Anne Radmacher

Many times when we think of courage we think of people who have accomplished great feats: military veterans, Olympic competitors, Freedom Riders of the '60s, explorers, astronauts and so on. Seldom do we add our names to this list.

We tend to think, "I've done nothing brave. I just survived a boring workday, listened to my spouse complain, and shelled out more money for school supplies. Tomorrow I'll do it all again: more boredom, more complaints, and more demands for money."

Actually, that is the whole point. Most of us can't learn what we need to know in one huge thunder boom. We have to learn it day by day. This is where the courage comes in. We need the courage to stick to the task, to try again tomorrow.

Our parents and grandparents survived the Great Depression and World War II. Most of us cannot imagine what their lives were like. Sometimes they told us stories that gave us hints of their desperation and courage to get out of bed one more day. Usually they talked about the fun things that happened when they were young. The lessons they taught us were:

"You have a job, be glad no matter what your duties."

"You have enough to eat, be glad even if you don't like it."

"Who cares if you have the latest style? You have more than one dress. Enjoy them."

We could go on and on about the things our parents taught us that we didn't want to hear. What they were saying and we did not hear was, "Sometimes courage is the quiet voice at the end of the day saying, 'Try again tomorrow.'"

We live in a world of instant gratification and forget that what we need to learn often takes longer than an instant, a day, or a year. Great art is not created in an hour; neither are great people. Take a moment to think about your personal heroes. Were they born with the innate ability to do what they did? Or did they have to learn from a skilled teacher or on their own? Did it take them a day or several months or years to become a masters at their trades?

One of my personal heroes is my granddaughter, Jennifer. She's a beautiful and smart young woman who works hard to raise her two sons to be polite, to do well in school and to have fun on their days off. This is a hard job for any of us. Doctors have never found a cause for the tremors that prevent her from doing everyday tasks like feeding herself with a fork or writing her name. Yet, every day she gets up, gets her boys off to school, and does what she can around the house. She works and shows up everyday rain or shine. Most of us would crawl under the covers and hide from the world and ask God to end our misery. Not Jennifer. She says, "I will try again tomorrow."

Another of my heroes is Jennifer's mother, who, in addition to her daily tasks, picks up the slack for her daughter, whatever that might entail. Linda also says, "I will try again tomorrow."

Can we do any less than these two courageous women?

Spirit, thank you so much for giving us another day to learn what we have to know. Thank you for giving us the courage to say "I will try again tomorrow."

CHANGE YOUR THOUGHTS, CHANGE YOUR LIFE.

"The only limit to our realization of tomorrow will be our doubts of today. Let us move forward with strong and active faith." - Franklin Delano Roosevelt

Many of us have based our lives on the premise that we must work hard and not waste our time daydreaming about what "could be" or "might be" or "hope to be." Our parents were young during the Roosevelt administration. They watched their parents struggle to feed them while their savings evaporated during the Great Depression and the Dust Bowl years. Our parents survived this terrible time and then were immediately called to serve in World War II.

They listened to the President's "fireside chats" on their radios and tried to believe the words he said. Most of them knew their only hope was to cling to his words, even though they didn't really believe them. In their hearts they knew that hard work with little reward was their lot in life. If they survived intact and saved a few dollars, they felt that they had done well.

Our parents taught us to save and live a quiet life that was a little better than theirs. If we could do that, then they felt that they had succeeded. Over the past 50 years our generation came to expect the finer things of life. Would we have the strength to survive what our parents experienced? Some of us, yes; some no. Fortunately, we don't have to learn that particular lesson, even though we still wonder why our children have to go to war and why millions of people perish daily from starvation.

Our lesson has been to learn the truth of Mr. Roosevelt's words. We now have many teachers writing books and telling us this same message day after day. We call it "Law of Attraction," "The Secret," "Change your Thoughts, Change your Life" and so many other beautiful words. It doesn't matter whose message resonates with us as long as we realize that the message is real. Many generations have known this truth.

These words, "The only limit to our realization of tomorrow will be our doubts of today. Let us move forward with strong and active faith," have been our guiding light for more than 400 years. If we look back through history, we can see that our nation was founded upon this truth. Later, our country split itself in two during the War Between the States, but it was rebuilt upon these words. And, so on through our generations.

While we see how these words have saved our country as it faced many crises, we also need to recall them as we face our own difficulties. Some of us have pretty good lives, while others struggle. Doubts keep us stuck in the cold and dark, and we don't like being there. Each of us needs to find his or her own path forward and then start moving along it.

Spirit, thank you for these words of wisdom, no matter their source. All holy writings teach the same lessons. Some have perverted those lessons to mean that only those who worship in a particular way will find the way out of physical or spiritual hardship. Please help us remember that each and every one of us, no matter what teachers we follow, is reading the same teachings and trying to "move forward with strong and active faith." Help us to find hope and the strong and active faith to move forward.

START AT THE BEGINNING

"All glory comes from daring to begin." -Eugene F. Ware

Often we look at a project and think that it is too large for us to handle. Maybe it is. But, just maybe, we are looking at the project as a completed whole rather than its component parts. Perhaps we can reach our goal if we take it in small increments. Most of life's accomplishments consist of many small steps.

At other times we look at the steps individually and think that some of them are too hard. What we fail to see is that step five will not be difficult if we just do steps one, two, three and four. In that way we build a base that will support our step five efforts. Then we can go on to steps six and beyond, because accomplishing step five has given us the confidence to do so. Each time we decide that a project is too large or complicated, we are limiting our abilities and our belief in ourselves. Deciding to tackle it anyway is a huge and scary step. Even so, deciding will not help us reach our goals. We have to take that first step, then the second and third.

Once a friend told me that I could have my house organized if I tackled the project for nine minutes a day. I found out that in nine minutes I can organize a drawer or toss out the towels that are so thin I can read a newspaper through them. Buying new ones is another nine-minute project. When enough nine-minute segments have been completed, so is the project.

Just think what confidence we can gain when we take each project a day at a time or even nine minutes at a time! As we see ourselves reaching our goal, we know that the next goal won't be so difficult. Soon we are confident and assured that we have the skills to do what needs to be done.

Spirit, I know that I can accomplish any goals I set for myself because You have promised that we can do whatever project is set before us. Please remind me each time I feel overwhelmed that with nine minutes a day, I can accomplish anything. When I remember this, I know all will be done on time and on budget. I know that this is so, because you have reminded us time and again that all is within our grasp. I claim that promise today.

CHANGE IS SCARY

"To keep our faces toward change and behave like free spirit sin the presence of fate is strength undefeatable." -Helen Keller

Change is scary even when it's for our highest good. We know where we are and think we know how the future will unfold, so most of us sit uncomfortably in our perceived fate and let life flow past us.

This is why we stay in jobs that bore us or demean us in some way. I'm not talking about what some people call menial labor, but about situations in which we are not respected professionally. We stay in those jobs because we think that we are assured a steady income and a nice retirement package. Recent events have shown that we can no longer count on working until retirement or even that the retirement funds will be available when we are ready to collect our benefits.

Other changes, like altering language or other bad habits can be stressful, so we continue these unhealthy mental or physical behaviors, even though we know that changing them would be good for us.

Then there are changes such as travelling to a place we've never been before, remodeling the kitchen, riding a zip line in our 60s, or even telephoning a new friend to suggest a get-acquainted meeting over coffee and cookies. Many people think that calling someone is easy and pleasurable. Other people think that punching those numbers on our cell phones, even to schedule a haircut, is effort equivalent to lifting an elephant.

Each of those activities requires a certain amount of risk. Do we stay where we think we are safe, or do we take that fearful step forward, knowing that the benefits may outweigh the risks?

No matter what we decide, change is inevitable. Why not make that change fit our requirements and dreams? As Helen Keller said, facing change is "strength undefeatable." So let's go for the strength and leave the fear on the road behind us.

Spirit, we know that you created us to feel fearless as well as fearful. The choice is ours. That decision will affect us for the rest of our lives, no matter what the result is. We can look at what appears to be a failure as a lesson learned or a signal to step backward. That too is our choice. Today we choose to accept a challenge to change, no matter how small or how large. Either way, we know that the experience will help us grow into the strong humans you created us to be.

ASK AND BE SURPRISED

"Ask for what you want. You just might get it. And…"

Two days ago I was scheduled to assist at a local hospital blood drive. I had an earlier appointment, so I arrived two hours late. I found the canteen in a mess: no cups, no napkins, and no recycling container. I asked my co-worker where those things were. She said, "This is all they gave us." This was true. The Red Cross only provides the basics, and the host site provides the nice touches.

I walked across the hall and asked a cafeteria worker if we could have some paper cups. She walked into the store room and returned with an unopened bag of plastic cups, just the right size for a little ice and a can of juice. I then went to the dining room accessory table and grabbed a stack of napkins. Then I asked one of the blood drive staff if he had an extra plastic bag I could use for recycling. He produced the perfect size bag. At the end of the afternoon I had a full bag of cans and cardboard containers to bring home and add to my bin.

My co-worker said, "You're a miracle worker. You just show up, and we get everything we need." I replied, "I'm not a miracle worker. I just asked if these items were available."

While I was slightly amused by the incident, I also felt sad for her. I used to be that way. When I was a child we were poor, so I learned quickly not to ask for things. My parents provided what they could; otherwise, I did without. They also told me not to ask others for things because it was not polite. When I married and was dissatisfied with our living conditions, an officer's wife told me, "If the Army wanted your husband to have a wife, they would have issued him one." In other words, don't complain or expect any favors.

A few years later I needed a new pair of shoes. My Keds were getting holes in the canvas. Finally, in frustration, I asked my husband why he didn't buy me a new pair. He said, "Why didn't you ask? I thought you liked wearing them that way."

After still more years, I was hired at a new job and given a tiny cubicle with a wobbly chair and a few worn out desk accessories. I used my own pens and pencils. One day I happened to ask my co-worker how she had acquired such nice office supplies when I had such poor quality items. She walked me over to the office supply cabinet and told me to help myself. I did, and she helped me carry my new supplies to my cubicle. When she saw my chair, she walked with me to the supervisor to ask for a new chair, which I received within a day. It turned out that my cubicle had been empty for some time, and people had just gotten into the habit of dumping their old things in there when they got new. "Ask for what you want" was beginning to soak into my brain.

A few years ago my mom (about 4 ft., 11 in tall) and I went to a public event and thought we had chosen a good viewing area. Just as the program was starting, a few very large men stepped in front of us and blocked our view. My mother became angry and said, "I guess he doesn't know he makes a better door than a window." I told her that they probably didn't even notice us since we were smaller than they. She replied, "Well, they could have looked around before they barged in." I tapped one of the men on the arm and asked, "Can my mother stand in front of you. She's short and can't see." The man smiled and said, "Of course, and you come up here too. I'm sorry. We just didn't notice you standing there." I thanked him, and we moved to the front and enjoyed the program.

Learning to ask for what I want was a long, slow process. But it works, even when what you want is intangible. I've learned to ask my Higher Power for things like safety, arriving where I'm going on time, friendship, and even groceries. All are provided when I remember to ask. A lesson from the Bible says simply, "Ask and it shall be given."

However, we cannot forget that asking is a two-part process. The second part is saying, "Thank you." All people and entities enjoy giving to people who appreciate their efforts, and they tend to feel used when those who ask don't express gratitude.

Spirit, thank you for giving me these words. I hope they will help someone find the courage to ask for what he or she needs.

FACE FEARFUL SITUATIONS

"Life is either a daring adventure or nothing." -Helen Keller

I've heard this quote many times over the years and thought I was living by its truth. However, I've come to realize that even though I've done many things that were unthinkable to others, I undertook many of those adventures because I was afraid of the alternative. This came to my attention recently and was reinforced the next morning in an email exchange with one of my role models.

A few days ago, some friends and I were talking about why our fondest wishes don't come true. We talked about trust, hope, determination, and more. Our conclusion was that we block our wishes with fear:

- fear that it won't happen,
- fear of what will happen if the wish does not come true,
- and fear of what will happen if the wish does come true.

We may not call it fear, but, instead, we use words like anxious, nervous, or concerned; however, the feeling is still fear to a greater-or-lesser degree. If we live in fear, our fears will come true. For example, if we're afraid we'll get a horrible disease, we will. If we fear that our boss won't give us the raise we deserve, she won't. If we fear our lover will be unfaithful, he will be. The same is true of the world at large. If we fear something bad will happen; i.e., famine, war, or disease, it will.

The next morning, I was having an e-mail conversation with my friend and bemoaning my lack of progress. She said, "Often I observe what others are doing and think I'm just standing still. But I plod along with purpose as you do, too."

Suddenly, I realized that I had not been plodding along with purpose but progressing in fits and starts. In between, I'd been living in fear, much less recently than in the past, but still with a certain amount of anxiety.

A few days ago my co-worker asked me to swap a shift with him. I said "NO! NO! NO!" and meant it with every fiber of my being. The next morning, I realized why I was so adamant about refusing to trade shifts with him. I had just been to his work station and had witnessed a scary (to me) event that was unlikely to ever happen again. I did not have a valid reason to be afraid. After realizing this, I told him that I would trade with him, and all went well on that shift.

The other side of fear is courage to take life one step at a time. Each day is a daring adventure if we face it without fear. We don't have to envision what life will be like "when." We just need to take life as it comes and be willing to try things we've never tried before. Wonderful experiences will grace our lives, perhaps even more than we had hoped.

Spirit, thank you for this reminder that we do not need to live in fear or even concern. We know that all will work out for our highest good if we trust that it will be so.

Chapter Four: Choices

DON'T DELAY

"Procrastination always delivers stress and disappointment…so what are you waiting for… do it now." -Window of Wisdom*

Life goes in cycles. Sometimes I'm focused on writing, sometimes on housework, and other times on yard work. Right now my focus is on the many inches of rain saturating this area, creating flood zones, and leaving our trees and homes vulnerable to the forces of Hurricane Joaquin that will be arriving in the next couple of days. I am wondering how we keep up with all our activities at once?

Some people seem to be able to juggle many balls at the same time. I struggle to keep one in the air at any given time. I have a million excuses for procrastinating. I'm:
- tired after working all day.
- choosing to spend time with the great-grandsons.
- wanting to write or finish a project.

The list is endless. As a result, I tend to feel like I'm not accomplishing anything important, like blogging on a regular basis.

Last year I had some health issues, nothing terrible, mostly annoying, but I just didn't feel up to home tasks. Work took all my energy. My health became good again, but I was feeling overwhelmed by all that needed to be done. Recently, I traveled to Niagara Falls and the surrounding area with Road Scholar. The trip was fantastic. When I arrived home with a huge pile of paperwork, souvenirs, and dirty laundry to add to the rest of the piles, my mind switched gears: I must organize. *Now.*

I spent part of one day just getting the vacation mess in order. The next day I spent several hours sorting my writing cabinet by "Things I've written," "Quotes and ideas," and "How to." I had been tossing everything into any drawer just to get it off my work table. After that I was able to slow down a bit. Now I'm focusing on one small task at a time.

A few years ago a wise woman told me to tackle tasks in nine-minute increments. She said that nine minutes would be enough to sort one drawer. Nine minutes each day would get my house organized in no time. That works for most things, but not my writing cabinet. But once I managed that task, I've been able to tackle one small task at a time. Yesterday, I picked up a small pile that had been hiding in a corner and found it to be last year's Christmas cards. Less than nine minutes took care of sorting them into cards to toss and cards from loved ones to keep.

Much of my time yesterday was spent moving plants and other items into my house and shed to protect them from the weather; shopping for nylon cord, water and batteries; and tying down large items. Even with that huge task plus working a short shift, I was able to sort the Christmas cards. My friend was right. Nine minutes was enough to take another step toward my end-goal of having an organized home and to feel good that I accomplished something useful.

I still have a lot of small piles. Most of what's in them can probably be filed in the recycling bin. Now I know they are manageable. Nine minutes a day really does save the stress level.

Spirit, thank you for showing me that I can accomplish more than I thought in just a few minutes a day. I still have much to sort and other tasks to tackle, but it now seems manageable. Also, I ask that you protect all areas potentially affected by this storm. I know that fear draws disaster, so I ask that you ease the fears of all who are located in the storm's path. Please show everyone what steps to take to prepare or evacuate as needed.

* "A Window of Wisdom," #907, September 27, 2015

LAUGH OR CRY

"Laughter is wine for the soul – laughter, soft or loud and deep-tinged through with seriousness ... the hilarious declaration made by man that life is worth living." -Sean O'Casey*

We often look at life as a serious situation. We're born, live a tough life, and then we die. What is there to laugh at? Everything.

My father was filled with anger and sadness, as were most men of his generation. They grew up during the Great Depression and survived horrendous circumstances in World War II. What was there to laugh at? Yet, if you attended any of our family reunions you would find the men outside under a shade tree laughing so hard that we could hear it from some distance away. What they found funny was a puzzle, because children were not privy to their conversations.

Sometimes we could talk them into going down to the creek with us to see what lurked under the water. While supposedly condescending to amuse the children, one of them would begin splashing us, and we all ended up in a big water fight. When called for dinner, we'd all slosh back up the hill and see our mothers standing on the porch laughing at us.

When asked how he was feeling, my dad would always respond, "With my fingers." He used to say that men didn't like skinny women. They wanted one "with a little meat on their bones." Invariably my mom would ask, "So why did you marry the skinniest woman in the county?" His response, "I fattened you up a bit, didn't I?"

As a child I couldn't understand why Dad was sometimes funny and sometimes angry. When I became an adult, I saw many of the same traits in myself and assumed it was an inherited disposition. As life progressed, I began to understand that on one level laughter was a coping mechanism. Dad was living that part of the quote, "tinged through with seriousness…"

As I grew older I began to learn about letting go of old pain. I found that the more pain I released, the more the quality of my laughter changed. Instead of laughing to release pain, I now laugh from pure joy. What a gift to laugh just because my great-grandsons give me hugs or because I see a friend! How joyous to laugh with delight because the sun is shining on my face and creating shadows under the trees. I'm so grateful that I've moved forward to "the hilarious declaration made by man that life is worth living."

While O'Casey didn't mention it, laughter is a great way to connect with others. Have you ever been in a meeting where everyone is working hard to protect his or her turf? You can feel that the people are disconnected from each other. Then someone tells a joke. As everyone laughs, the distance melts and the group begins to work as a team.

Spirit, thank you for the gift of laughter and learning that laughter can help us in so many ways. It can release pain. It is a way to connect with others. It is a way to express joy. We laugh with joy that we are alive, while we laugh at the funny things humans do every day.

* Originally John O'Casey (1880-1964), Irish playwright, Green Crows, "Saturday Night," 1956

ALLOW CHANGES

"The way to start changing your mind is not to force it or command it, but to watch it." -Martha Beck*

Many of us have been told since we were small children that if we want something we need to work hard and stay focused. True, but that tactic often leads to frustration rather than to obtaining peace of mind.

I've learned the hard way that when I want to change my behavior, I do not succeed on determination alone. For example, I may decide to exercise more and even purchase a gym membership. But I seldom go to the gym unless I have an exercise partner who keeps reminding me that it's workout day.

However, if I say to myself and the Universe, "I'd like to get more exercise," and not worry about how that will happen, I find that situations arise that require muscle use. Perhaps a storm comes and I need to rake the yard and carry debris to the compost pile. Possibly, I'll need a small item or two from the store. I usually say, "That's not worth driving the car. I'll walk to the store."

The same applies to eating healthy food. If I decide to diet, all sorts of tempting yummies pop up in front of my face and call my name. If I say, "I choose healthy eating," and release the outcome, I find that my food choices are healthier, even when tempting desserts are on the table.

One of my biggest problems was to see certain people in the light of what they did to me. That trait caused me mental and physical anguish over the years. What we think about becomes evident in our bodies with chronic headaches, back aches, compulsive eating and other issues. So how do we reverse those situations and let go of the physical pain? We must realize that we choose to experience our life as it is. I know this gets into the woo-woo view of life, but I've found it makes sense.

For example, I was married twice – to jerks. Whose decision was that? Mine. Different people suggested that perhaps these men were not the best choices, but I chose not to listen. Unhappy work experiences – the same. Just because a job pays more money doesn't mean it will give more satisfaction. An unhappy person tends to take it out on others. Then those people react in kind. These events seemed to prove that everyone was conspiring to make me miserable.

Eventually, I learned that my thoughts and actions were creating my unpleasant experiences. When I became aware that, just perhaps, my complaining caused people to dislike my company, I asked the Universe to help me complain less. When I realized that I had an option other than to fear what awaited me at home, I asked myself if there was a way to leave the situation.

As far as my parents were concerned, well, they treated me better than they had been treated. I repeated the "tradition" with my children. Even though I became aware of other options, I just didn't know how to implement them. Sometimes I was so frustrated by life that I took it out on the children. Just knowing that there were other ways to raise children gave me the impetus to change. I told myself and the Universe that I wanted to be a better parent. Parenting books came to my attention. School counselors suggested a better way. Little by little, I improved my skills. I still made a lot of mistakes, but I must have changed some, because my adult children are now an important part of my life.

Situations don't come into our lives to give us grief, even though it often seems that way. Events happen to help us grow into the people we are capable of being. It's our choice how we respond to those events. We can fall into the "poor me" pit, or we can choose to find a solution. I know this is true, because I spent many years in that nasty pit. It was only when I wanted to find a way out that I began to see a little blue sky here or a ray of sun there. I was able to start climbing up to the surface. I'm not dancing on sunshine yet, but I'm beginning to hear a few notes from the band.

I used a lot of words to say that when you want to change, the easiest way is to state your problem to yourself and the Universe. Part two is not to worry about how and to release the outcome. Step three is to do something else while you are waiting for the miracle. Mike Dooley expressed it well in a recent message from the

Universe: "Often the very most spiritual thing one can do is get busy. Physically busy. Hoeing, chopping, planting. Connecting, moving, grooving. Dipping, swirling, twirling…" **

Spirit, sometimes we are sunk in despair up to our necks and see no way out. We ask you to show us how to move from fear and anger toward joy. We know it may be a short step or it could be a long walk. Either way, we know that if we ask for an option it, will come into our awareness and prompt us to necessary action.

*Beck, Martha, Daily Inspiration, info@marthabeck.com, February 26, 2016

**Dooley, Mike, TUT – A note from the Universe, theuniverse@tut.com, March 4, 2016

WRONG ROAD?

"...Two roads diverged in a wood, and I-I took the road less traveled by, and that has made all the difference. -Robert Frost*

As we travel through our days, sometimes the road is a smooth, easy ride. At other times, we hit small bumps or potholes that damage our egos and indicate that we are traveling the wrong road and need to make a detour sooner rather than later. With no change, we can keep driving down that road until our car is wrecked and our souls are bleeding.

Why do we continue this disastrous pattern? Often we don't see another road that we can travel. Or we see an alternate road but are afraid to make the turn because the old road is familiar. We know where the bumpy road will take us. We don't know what will happen if we change direction.

Those fears are valid. We don't know where the new road will lead. Often we are taught from childhood that we must follow a certain path, no matter what. Fear of change can be a generational roadblock. Other parents teach their children to go for the prize. A friend once told me that he was taught to shoot for the stars, and if he only reached the moon, he'd still be further than if he had remained Earth-bound.

My own upbringing was more along the fearful lines. If I were to step out of my role, something terrible would happen. I would live to regret my rash behavior. I believed that for many situations, like speaking up at work, but sometimes I took chances and am glad I did. I had to change my direction several times. While many decisions had serious repercussions, these always came with gifts that made my life better. Some examples:

My first marriage was a disaster, but my three wonderful children made life worthwhile.

I left that marriage not knowing what might happen, but I learned that I was capable of earning a living for my young family.

After my children were grown, I enrolled in an elite college with only $25 dollars in my pocket. I graduated at age 47 with less student debt than anticipated. That degree led to better jobs.

At 55, I chose early retirement and a severely-reduced benefit to move across the country to live near my daughters. That move allowed me to watch my grandchildren reach adulthood and give me four great-grandsons that are the delight of my life. And, another baby is on the way!

In 2013 my favorite online inspirational writer chose to close her blog. Uncharacteristically, I chose to continue her work with "Thoughts to Ponder." While my following is not as large as hers, the number is growing. And now I am publishing my first book.

Most of all, I feel satisfaction in doing my part to make the world a more peaceful place.

All that is a long way to say that it is never too late to change your direction. I'm now looking for other ways to expand my life and new roads to travel. If I don't fly among the stars, I'm still a lot further than if I'd never started this journey. I urge you to take a risk and take "the road less travelled." You may face some unpleasant situations, but you will have gained so much more.

Spirit, thank you for showing us that we have options. We can change directions as often as necessary to reach our goals. By exploring new roads, we learn that we have talents we never expected. Those talents will lead us down more roads to new adventures. Those choices might not all lead to the stars, but they will certainly get us further on our journey than if we stay focused on the potholes in front of us.

*Frost, Robert, "The Road Not Taken," in *Mountain Interval*, 1916.

NO EXCUSES

"The long and the short of it goes something like this: When one stops looking for the quick-and-easy way and just deals with what's on their plate, the quick-and-easy way soon finds them. Actually, what could be quicker than beginning with where you are or easier than starting with what you've got?" -TUT, a note from the Universe.

Wow! Those words put us on the spot, don't they? The author is saying, "No more excuses." How many of us are saying, at this very moment, "I'll follow my dream – when I have more time, money, energy, clean socks and have memorized the dictionary," or, "I'll go to the beach after I retire."

This procrastination also applies to ordinary daily tasks: "I'll do the dishes after I check email." "I'll go for a walk after I finish the laundry." How about walking while the washing machine is doing its work? There are so many ways we use excuses to delay living life to the fullest. Yet, we know that if we just do it, the task is smaller and time goes faster than we thought.

The TUT quote says to begin with where we are, wherever that is. Barbara Brown Taylor carries that thought further:

"If you are in the dark, it does not mean that you have failed and that you have taken some terrible misstep. For many years I thought my questions and my doubt and my sense of God's absence were all signs of my lack of faith, but now I know this is the way the life of the spirit goes." *

Spirit, thank you for these messages that keep popping into our awareness, just when we need them most. Often they come from surprising sources. Please open our hearts and minds to absorb the messages that can lead us to a better life. We can't always know where or what that better life is. We ask that you give us the courage to follow the prompting, whether it is a big neon sign or a barely audible whisper in our ears.

*TIME magazine, April 28, 2014

CHOOSE LOVE

"We can do no great things – only small things with great love."
-Mother Teresa

I'm writing this on election day. Hooray! I'm so tired of listening to candidates brag about all the great things they'll do for us if we just elect them to be – whatever they want to be. In reality, they can only do great things if they can persuade their cohorts to go along with their plans.

Let's bring this idea back to us. We want to solve everyone's problems, cure everyone's illnesses, make our teens stop arguing, and dogs stop chasing cats. We could do that if only everyone would listen to our sage advice. Our lives may be in chaos, but we know exactly what other people should do. We tell them loudly and often how to improve their lives and wonder why they don't listen to us.

Most of us have left that controlling person behind and have focused our energy in other directions – learning healing skills and getting degrees in a variety of helping professions, for example. With this knowledge, we just "know" we can help others, and we do.

Until one day a person we care about needs our help. We try, but we are so concerned with proving how good we are that the improvement fails to manifest. Eventually we realize that we tried to do great things to impress that person. At this point, we must remember to leave our egos behind and confront each small thing with great love.

Love is everything. That's why we admire Mother Teresa and why she has been elevated to sainthood. Each of us can be a Mother Teresa in our own small worlds. We may not be nominated for sainthood, but our loved ones will benefit from our work.

Spirit, we thank you for giving us a role model like Mother Teresa. She clearly showed us how to live our lives with great love. With your guidance we can do just that as we remember that love is superior to works. Thank you for reminding us that love really does make the world go around. We choose to live our lives doing small things with great love.

ATTITUDE CHOICE

"A major advantage of age is learning to accept people without passing judgment." -Liz Carpenter*

Most of us have learned to judge people by their age, size, color, wealth, education and many other non-specific criteria that we have stashed away in our minds. Often we harshly judge those who don't meet our standards. At other times, we can dismiss those differences with a "different strokes for different folks" attitude. Being able to accept other people for who they are is an attitude most of us cultivate.

Today, however, I want to discuss a more difficult challenge – accepting ourselves where we are each and every moment. Most of us have learned to accept ourselves most of the time. Periodically, we still denigrate ourselves with "shoulda, woulda, coulda". To some extent, that is just human nature. We have a choice. We can live with and nurture our petty complaints, or we can look at the big picture. We're alive. We're functioning to whatever ability we have and are able to feel empathy for others.

This last was a choice I denied myself yesterday. I woke up feeling deprived, abused, neglected and generally in a sorry mood. I was upset because over the past few years I've had some health issues, annoying and inconvenient, but in the larger view, rather petty. I ranted at my God, angels, guides, and whomever else might have been listening. "I'm tired of all these health issues! If I had the energy I could have done this activity. If I hadn't had to spend so much money on medications, physical therapy and dental work, I could have gone on this trip or have done that project. I'm angry. I want to spend my time and energy on having fun, not on health issues." The worst part was that I shared my anger with a kind young man whose mother can't eat solid food. I'm sure she wishes that her health issues were as minor as mine.

This morning I awoke with a lesson that I've shared here in the past, but it had been floating around in my miasma of anger and fear. Yes, fear. If I'm this decrepit now, what will life be like in another ten years? The truth is, I probably have another twenty or more years to learn what life holds for me.

The most important lesson is that we cannot change who and what we are until we accept who and what we are today, in this very moment. I had to accept that I was angry over relatively easy-to-handle problems. The doctor sent me to physical therapy to relieve what has turned out to be temporary pain. If I didn't spend money on therapy, I may have eventually lost the use of my arm. What would have that cost? My recent bout with breathing issues is healing with prescription medications. What would have been the cost without that option? Expensive dental work provided me with a new tooth. What would have been the long-term cost of not being able to eat crunchy food?

Each of us faces his or her own personal issues to complain about and accept or not accept. We all have our personal heroes who have borne difficulties that we can only imagine, yet they triumphed in life. Helen Keller and Steven Hawking are two who come immediately to mind. Keller was deaf and blind, yet she blossomed into a woman whom we often quote for inspiration. Hawking cannot control his body, but his brain continues to astound us on a regular basis. They continue to inspire us to move forward, no matter what. As long as life is, we have hope.

Spirit, thank you for putting our problems in perspective. Thank you for showing us that acceptance and gratitude are the basis for a happy life. Thank you for giving us the ability to see the positive outcomes of our negative experiences. Thank you for giving us another day to live in gratitude.

*Carpenter, Liz, The Treasury of Women's Quotations, pg. 20, Carolyn Warner, Prentiss Hall, 1992

SPEND TO EARN

"All expenditures, whether from the heart or the wallet, in the past or present, big or small, can be viewed as either 'depleting' or 'enriching.' Enriching works for me." -The Universe *

Many of us were raised with the idea that we have to hold on to our physical, mental and spiritual resources, or we will lack what we need to live a good life. If we give away too much time, money, or love, we will run out of that resource. The opposite is true. We must be willing to give of ourselves to enrich ourselves.

I'm not suggesting that we drain our bank accounts to build a homeless shelter or quit our jobs to become the second Mother Teresa. I am suggesting that we be a little more generous to those who might need a boost. Donating money or goods is beneficial, but we can give in other ways as well.

We can give by listening with our hearts and our minds to the message behind a person's words. Once we understand what is happening behind the words, we can provide a better response. The second part of that is to accept that person just where he or she is. This is often hard when we see that person's potential or what we consider to be a waste of their talents.

We might want to ask our guides to tell us how to respond. Possibly we can steer the other person to a job opportunity, a doctor, or a helpful resource. Perhaps the person just wants to be heard and to hear us say, "I understand," without telling our own story. This is hard for me. I love to relate my own tale of woe or joy and have stories for any situation.

We might send up a quick, silent prayer for that person's highest good. It's not our place to ask God to heal their illness, provide them a job, or send them a free car. We don't know what lesson they need to learn or what gifts they may receive by walking their current path. By asking for their highest good, we're allowing what is needed to be given and received.

We should be enriching ourselves in the same way. We can prepare for any situation that may come our way by saying each morning, "Today I choose to be the best me that I can be." Whatever entity we consider to be our Higher Power will understand what we need and give us those resources or talents. If we don't believe in a Higher Power, that's okay too. Our inner selves will hear and steer us in the right direction.

Either way, we will grow bit by bit into better humans, so we can spend more on others and enrich ourselves in the process. This is reflected in the way Dooley ends his daily message, "Thoughts become things… choose the good ones! ®" *

Spirit, today I ask that you give me the inspiration, motivation, energy and resources to be the best I can be and do the things I need and want to do and to enjoy each moment as it occurs!

*Mike Dooley, TUT - A Note from the Universe, www.tut.com, August 19, 2015

CHOOSE HOW WE ACT

"I've learned that people will forget what you said, people will forget what you did, but people will never forget how you made them feel." -Maya Angelou

This is not a tribute to Dr. Angelou, though I'd be glad to add my praise to all the others who've taken the time to write about her impact on their lives. I'll just say that she gave me courage to keep on keeping on.

Her quote explains how most of us got to where we are today. Our station in life often reflects how people have made us feel over the years. Retrospectives are a pain, but they often teach us what we need to know today.

Did our parents, teachers, friends and spouses let us know they valued our presence, knowledge and love?

Or did they show us that we were a nuisance, substandard and a drain on their emotions, money and time?

Did they just ignore us and pretend we didn't exist?

We've all felt valued, or devalued and ignored. Which of those feelings dominated our lives and made us the people we are today? How do we treat other people? Do we value, devalue, or ignore them? How will our actions impact those people as they go out into the world?

No matter how we have been treated in the past, we can determine to be better people. We have a choice about how we treat ourselves. Are we kind, considerate, and forgiving of ourselves? How we treat ourselves is reflected in how we treat others.

As someone once said, "God don't make junk. So don't act like you are."

Creator Spirit, thank you for the gift of life and the ability to evaluate our actions and how they've been impacted by our experiences. We thank you that you've given us the ability to learn and improve. We choose to be messengers of love, kindness and thoughtful action that bring peace and confidence to those we meet on our journey.

GOOD MOOD OR BAD

"The most important decision you make is to be in a good mood." -Voltaire

We can decide to have a good mood!

This is a shock to many of us who grew up believing that our moods were dictated to us. We learned to reflect the moods of those around us. As children, that meant our parents and teachers. We were we told, "You should be happy, because..." Or, "Why are you happy? Just look at what is happening..." The pattern repeated itself as we matured. We learned to feel what we thought we were supposed to feel.

This is not to say that we shouldn't empathize with those around us. Empathy is a gift to us as well as to others, but we don't need to wallow in another's pain.

Eventually, we began learning and integrating the revolutionary idea that we could feel how we felt. We finally gave ourselves permission to feel happy when others were sad – and to feel sad when others were happy.

We can choose to be in a good mood, no matter what is happening in our surroundings. We don't need to mask our true feelings, but we can avoid getting sucked into another's vortex of despair.

We learn that most of the time our good mood is contagious to us as well as to others. Perhaps we wake up in a good mood because we slept well. We can hang on to that thought even though traffic is making us late for work or, or, or... As the day progresses, we will notice that our good mood extends itself. We still feel good at the end of the day.

Best of all, good moods are contagious. Often a smile and a simple "thank you" are enough to lift another person from the doldrums. If not, well, there is always the next person.

Creator Spirit, thank you for the gift of joy, the gift of knowing that we are happy inside even if others are not. We know that being in a good mood is an extension of gratitude. If we are grateful, a good mood naturally follows. Good moods are contagious!

LOOK AT POSSIBILITIES

"Anything is possible. Stay open, forever, so open it hurts, and then open up some more, until the day you die, world without end, amen." -George Saunders*

This week I've been a bit under the weather, so I am offering you a few bits of wisdom I've picked up here and there. I originally thought this might be a mid-year resolution list, but I know living in the moment is more important. Besides, resolutions don't work unless you think you are worthy of the outcome.

Here are some thoughts from modern teachers:

Dr. Phil McGraw – Words to live by in 2014*
"Everybody has a personal truth. A strong sense of self is the foundation. A successful reinvention happens when you love yourself enough to believe you can do better and deserve better. The Universe rewards action. The major difference between a dream and a goal is a timeline for progress ... (and) accountability. We generate the results we believe we deserve."

Martha Beck's Plan for finding joy*
"Have a vision. Let go of what doesn't work. Don't be afraid to fail. Pay attention to what really matters to you."

Brené Brown - Dare to play*
"Create a play list - activities you could do for hours on end. Carve out time on your calendar. Protect playtime the way you protect work. Play well with others – do things that make us all our most silly, creative, and free-spirited selves."

Iyanla Vanzant – How do I break a negative pattern? *
"Notice it. Know its cause. Slow down! ... To see things for what they really are. Forgive yourself. Check in ... What am I doing and why?"

Creator Spirit, thank you for these wise people who offer their knowledge to us. We know that there are many more teachers circling us daily. We know, but sometimes deny, that we are teachers too, sometimes for good, sometimes for bad. Please show us how to step into our truth and be the best teachers we can be.

*All of the quotes come from the January, 2014, "O, the Oprah magazine."

WHAT YOU REALLY WANT

"You draw to you the essence of whatever you are predominately thinking about. So if you are predominately thinking about the things you desire, your life experience reflects those things. And, in the same way, if you are predominately thinking about what you do not want, your life experience reflects those things." -Esther and Jerry Hicks

This quote is difficult to understand and even harder to put into practice. Our society has taught us to worry and complain. Some say, "To worry is to show love." News sources concentrate on what is wrong in this world – war, disasters, crooked politicians, murder, new diseases…

We seldom hear about what is going right – happy, honest people; a country at peace; a day without a homicide; a new cure without dangerous side effects, for example.

Do you see that I just negated the power of the quote by complaining? Even an explanation can remove the power of positive thinking. Once we figure out how to keep our thoughts aligned with our desires, we can live the life we desire. We need details, but probably not too many details. When we tell the Universe what we'd like to experience, we can cancel the request by thinking too much.

For example, we want to buy a house, and we tell the Universe that we want two bedrooms, ground floor only, a lot of trees, and a lot of windows to enjoy looking at the trees. The Universe starts looking for a home to meet our desires. Then we start thinking instead of trees, we'd like to have a swimming pool. The Universe has to cancel the first search and start all over again. Then we begin to worry that the neighbors will take advantage of our kindness and use our pool daily.

So what do the Universe and the real estate agent present to us? How about a single floor home with two bedrooms, many windows, a pool and greedy neighbors? Our wish was granted!

These thought patterns can affect us in other ways. A friend related a story about one of her friends who was driving to work and wishing she didn't have to work at that business any more. She arrived at work and was handed a layoff notice – effective immediately. Her wish was granted.

If she had thought about what occupation would satisfy her more, she would have started seeing ads for jobs in the new occupation and would have heard of openings through the job grapevine. Then she could have been hired and would have been able to give her notice, making a smooth transition from one job to the next. Her wish would have been granted in a more satisfactory way.

Another example is that we don't want to visit relatives and we wake up with the flu. Our wish is fulfilled, but not the way we want. What if we say, "We'd rather play golf today than visit relatives?"

To learn the skill of receiving what we want, we start by monitoring our thoughts. If we notice our thoughts going down Don't Want Street, we can void those thoughts and get back on track. We need to remind ourselves gently not to say, "I'm so hungry I could eat a bear," when we actually want a cheeseburger.

Universe, please make me aware when my thinking meanders into the "don't want" column. Show me how to bring my thinking back into the "do want" column. Show me how to phrase my request so I receive what I want and need. Guide me gently through the learning process until I am communicating clearly and living the life that I was born to live.

PRAY JOYFULLY

"You pray in your distress and in your need: would that you might pray also in the fullness of your joy and in your days of abundance." -Kahlil Gibran

As Master Gibran said, we do pray in our distress and need: We pray to be healed. We pray for a better house or a life partner who truly loves us. We pray that our children remain healthy and get into a good college. We pray that we have enough money to pay for that college.

All of those reasons and so many more are why we pray in fear, distress, need, or what we think we need. Indeed, these are worthy of our prayer efforts; but do fearful, needy prayers work? Sometimes.

But what would happen if our prayers focused on gratitude instead? Are we grateful for the sunrise, our jobs that drive us crazy, our children who are acting out, or a lazy, spendthrift life partner? This is not always easy. Sometimes our lack of gratitude isn't because of life circumstances. Rather this lack is often a clue that we have not let go of guilt or even stupid decisions. In other words, we are angry at ourselves.

Perhaps we are so consumed with our grievances that we don't even notice, much less appreciate, the anniversary flowers or our child's scholastic achievement. If our employer gives a raise, we don't feel gratitude, but think that the raise is long overdue and too small.

What if we focus on those things that give us joy? Does a child's smile make us feel warm and fuzzy inside? Do we notice that the birds are singing? Did the traffic clear enough so we arrived at work on time? These are small things to be sure. Are they worthy of gratitude? Definitely.

But we say our lives are too miserable to be grateful. Are they? Someone once said, "Fake it until you make it." You may not feel grateful, but say thank you anyway. That's not lying. Faking gratitude gives us a hint of what real gratitude feels like when it arrives. Living in gratitude is a gift that cannot be surpassed by any earthly gift.

Spirit, we thank you for the new day, the trees, plants, flowers, animals, birds, and nature spirits. We thank you for all we will experience today. We thank you that we have a job that pays the bills, even if we don't like it, because we are learning valuable work and coping skills. We thank you that our children smiled as they ran out the door to catch the school bus. We thank you that we made stupid decisions to marry the wrong people because those mistakes gave us those precious children. We thank you that our parents are ill and need help. Our time with them is a wonder. They tell us things we never knew before, like they were proud of us even though we were convinced that they were ashamed of us.

Thank you, Spirit, for life and all experiences because you have promised us that all is as it should be. You also said that if we are grateful for the small things, our big dreams will be fulfilled as well. You have promised us joy, and we accept it into our lives today.

STEP OFF THE CLIFF

"Nobody can go back and start a new beginning, but anyone can start today and make a new ending." -Maria Robinson

Some of us have lived several decades, others only a few years. Most of us have regrets. Some allow those regrets to shape our lives. Others have allowed "words of wisdom" to forever shape their lives and futures.

Our thoughts have influenced our decisions, sometimes for good or bad. My dad used to say, "Once you are in debt, you are always in debt." That was his experience. However, after his retirement he and my mom sold their tiny house and moved into a low-income senior community. They paid all their bills and paid cash for their first new car. They were able to take a few budget vacations and live more comfortably. While their life seemed Spartan to others, it was good for them. Retirement allowed them to make a new beginning.

A few years ago a relative I hadn't seen for many years made contact. While reconnecting was a joyful experience, I couldn't help feeling sad for her. During that and subsequent conversations, she stated firmly, "---- has always been this way and will always be this way." She had experienced unpleasant events and was filled with anger.

She was convinced that since these situations had been her past, they would be her future, not allowing new experiences to come into her life. The last time I saw her, another disaster had befallen her family and she was bowed under the weight of more responsibility. I hope that the fairies will clean her window so she can see a brighter future.

Life was similar for me for many decades. I saw life as one crisis after another with little happiness between. Even joyful events seemed to have time limits. However, something within me encouraged me to take a risk and then another and another. Some brought me a measure of joy, and some brought painful lessons. Yet, the past 15 years have shown me that lasting change doesn't have to do with events, but with thoughts. We can choose either to feel trapped or to see a path leading into a sunnier future. Not all my choices have turned out as I wished, but they all led me forward. This last year, I've faced several minor health crises that initially made me feel afraid. However, as I proceeded through diagnoses and treatments, I saw that each crisis resolved a long-standing health issue, allowing me to move forward with more energy and enthusiasm.

For example, a few weeks ago I saw a podiatrist for an ingrown toe nail. She provided standard treatment and asked a few questions. She then added a pad to my arch support that allows me to stand straighter. Not only is my toe healing without stress, but also my steps are straighter and more sure. No more wobbling. No more fear of falling.

Last evening during meditation my guides took me on a trip. The details aren't important. The lesson is. They showed me that it is safe to step off a cliff, metaphorically speaking. If I'm brave enough to take that next step, adventure and joy will follow. Just as my health issues are resolving themselves day by day, my courage can also grow if I let it. When my courage grows, my joy grows.

Creator Spirit, thank you for these lessons, even those that come with bumps and bruises. Each lesson brings us closer to learning that peace, love and joy are all there are. You are showing us that we can only experience the best life has to offer if we are brave enough to take that next step, whatever it might be. Open our windows to the world and show us that our past does not have to be our future.

FRET OR FOCUS

"The focus of our own behavior should be our primary focus." - Window of Wisdom1

"The energy we lose in fretting we would gain with a smile." - Pamela Harper2

How often do we think or say, "Work would be wonderful if it wasn't for my coworker who rambles on and on at staff meetings and my boss who expects miracles?" Or perhaps, "My marriage would be wonderful if only my husband/wife wasn't such a jerk?" It may be true that our coworker, boss and life partner are complete and total jerks. If they are, there is nothing that we can do to change them. We either have to accept their behaviors or move on to something better.

Of course, our own behaviors are exemplary. Don't we wish? An old saying goes something like, "For every finger we point at someone else, four are pointing back at us." Pointing fingers seems to be our primary occupation. We love to criticize everyone and everything that is contrary to what we believe.

While we are pointing our fingers, we are also fretting about how the other person's behavior is going to affect us. We think that their misbehavior will reflect badly on us. Most likely it won't, but if it does, we won't be held responsible.

We also fret about all sorts of things that will most likely never happen. "If I buy a new car, some fool will put a dent in it." True. Eventually, all cars get dents and scratches. "If I tell the doctor about my stomach ache, he or she will put me in the hospital and run all sorts of tests." Possibly, and just as probably, the doctor will tell you that your stomach hurts because you're eating something that isn't good for you. All you have to do is eliminate that item and all will be well. I know, that particular food is delicious and life will be miserable without it. However, we just might learn to like celery if we smile when we eat it.

I've been fretting a lot lately about health issues. Nothing is seriously wrong. I just have several minor issues that need attention.

I'm not fretting that I have a terrible condition. I'm fretting because my issues require temporary exercise and outdoor limitations. The weather is beautiful, and I want to be outside having fun this time of year. I'm fretting and pouting about something very minor in the larger view of life experiences. Yet to me, they seem gigantic, and fretting is draining the energy I could be using for something productive, even if it is inside the house. I might think, "This will give me time to dust the ceiling fan." Yeah, right!

At the same time, I'm pointing my finger at my health care providers because their treatments are causing my short-term discomfort. My health care providers did not cause these issues; my own carelessness did. Over the years I have been careless about following their advice, so now I'm paying the price. Luckily, the price is very low when compared to what other people endure. I'm grateful that my discomfort is minor, and I want it to stay that way.

As a result, I'm asking my guides gently to remind me to accept the blame for my problems, to care for my health (and other issues), and to stop thinking that anything else is more important. It's hard to face, but these are steps I must take. I cannot blame my old behaviors on anyone but myself, and fretting about the results harms no one but me. Well, except for the people who have to listen to me complain!

Spirit, today I choose to smile rather than to fret. We know that each situation that appears in our lives provides us with an opportunity to grow into a better person. Thank you for giving us these opportunities.

EMOTIONAL DISCOMFORT

"Emotional discomfort, when accepted, rises, crests, and falls in a series of waves. Each wave washes parts of us away and deposits treasures we never imagined. No one would call it easy, but the rhythm of emotional pain that we learn to tolerate is natural, constructive, and expansive. It's different from the sting of decay; the pain leaves you healthier than it found you." -Martha Beck*

This quote came at the perfect time.

This afternoon I received my Alverno College alumnae magazine. As those publications do, it highlighted outstanding alumnae and their achievements. I'm extremely proud that I graduated from this top-ranked college in only five years at the age of 47 while working full-time. That schedule precluded participating in student events and making close friends, a part of the "normal" college experience. However, my BA degree allowed me to earn promotions that previously would have been out of my reach. Yet reading the magazine, I wondered if they were proud of me. A profound sadness fell over me as I thought they would not be.

A series of life choices led me to attend Alverno at that particular time in my life. I married shortly out of high school basically to leave home and my hometown. My husband and I had some fun, some tough times, and three wonderful children. But over the years I determined that this was not what I wanted from life and left the marriage, taking the children with me.

Life as a single mother was hard but rewarding. Other experiences led me down a path that was often enjoyable and sometimes miserable. At one point after college, I was working three part-time jobs. All were interesting and great learning experiences, but not where I anticipated I'd be after college.

Then came the day when all my children and sons-in-law were out of the military and had settled lives. I decided to retire at age 55 and move to Virginia so I could get to know my adult daughters, their husbands, and children while they were still young. This was the best decision of my life. In addition to being family, we all became friends. Now I adore my four great-grandsons. If I had waited until age 65 to retire, all these loving family members would be strangers. There are times when I think I'm more of a burden than a contributor to them, but that is my impression to correct.

Since I moved here I've had some exciting jobs and some depressing jobs. My current jobs are excellent for retired people, but not for career building. At this point in my life, I do not want to build a career. I want to experience peace, love and joy and meet interesting people along the way. I have met some dear friends and teachers. I wish we could be closer friends. Whose fault is that? Definitely mine, because I hesitate to reach out to them. Instead I sit at home and wish they would call me.

All this is a long way to say that I've experienced every word of Martha Beck's quote. I know that all she said is true. As I look back on my various experiences, I can see the highs, lows, pains and lessons they presented. Every experience taught me something I needed to learn.

Today's lesson is to accept all my experiences, even those that seem to be terrible mistakes. I must accept myself where I am today. It is never too late to begin a new phase or a new adventure.

Spirit, I ask you to hold me to that knowledge and not let me waste my time fretting and moaning!

Chapter Five: Stronger than We Think

READY, SET, GO!

"There are two simple truths you need to accept if you are to move effortlessly into the world of soul, the world which is based on the laws of love: You are Ready. You are Holy." -Rev. Angela Peregoff*

When I read these words, my first thought was, "Yeah, right!" You may be thinking the same thing. But just a few days later, Rev. Angela announced her retirement from "Morning Blessings." The news devastated me. I had relied on Rev. Angela's morning messages for several years. What would I do now? Where would I get my daily guidance?

She was moving on to a new chapter in her life, and I could do nothing about it. I took a break from grieving and said a prayer for Rev. Angela's highest good. Just as I finished, my guide said, "It's your turn."

But I don't have her credentials! I don't have her following! I don't know what to say!

My guide just chuckled and asked, "Will you trust me to guide you?"

What could I say but yes? I'm not dumb enough to tell my guide no. I spent too many years thinking I was the smartest kid on the block and it didn't get me anywhere. Eventually, the truth sunk into my little pea brain: When I succeeded, I wasn't in the driver's seat. I had, of necessity, let go of the details. And what do you know? It worked.

My guide told me that I could start on a smaller scale, perhaps writing once a week. In the meanwhile, I should start reading some of the holy books that I had piled around the house, and, most importantly, trust my guide and work from a place of love.

Is the guide's name, Jesus? Is he or she a saint? An angel? An Ascended Master? My son who crossed over 16 months ago? I don't know, but I am inclined to think "all of the above." The label is not important to me. I use them all at different times.

The important message for me is to listen and take action. Rev. Angela said, "You are ready," and "You are holy." I'm ready because I received the message. Am I holy? Well, I'm not sure about that, but I do know that if I follow directions with love, not pride, some of my actions and words will be holy.

I didn't intend this message to be about me, but as I began typing, my guide said, "Perhaps your reader is asking the same questions. Write about your doubts and that you took the first step anyway. A reader will understand that he or she also is ready and holy."

Spirit, please guide us to find the paths we are to follow. Give us the courage to take that first step and the willingness to act on the messages you send us. We thank you for your eternal patience with our doubts and fears. We thank you for staying beside us every day, even when we aren't listening. We choose to accept your challenge to be ready and holy, whatever that means.

* Excerpt from Reverend Angela Peregoff's "Morning Blessings," March 29, 2013

TRUST YOURSELF

"The most common way people give up their power is by believing they don't have any." Celie in *The Color Purple* by Alice Walker

The first time I read *The Color Purple*, I wept for Celie, the victim. By the time I read it a third and fourth time, I saw that she really had more power than I thought. Even though I finally saw Celie's power and bravery, I did not see that I had any.

We are born with power, but many of us are taught in our early years that we must never access that power. We learn our lessons the hard way. Celie certainly did. She was a classic victim, taught by her step-father, her husband and society that she had no power. Cinderella had the handsome prince to rescue her, but Celie did not, nor do we.

This awareness can come to us in a moment, or it may take many years to soak into our consciousness. We have many options now. We can believe in our personal power. We can believe that a Higher Power protects us. Any way that we tune into our strength is perfect. We learn to take a deep breath and calmly evaluate the situation. Then we can determine what a reasonable response is.

Often we can talk our way out of a situation that does not serve our highest good. Sometimes we need to run. Whatever message we get from our intuition is correct. We need to learn to trust that inner voice and take proper action. After we protect ourselves and our children a few times the message will finally sink into our clouded brains: We are powerful beings. We know what is best for us and our families.

Celie learned this lesson over a period of many years. We have more access to the outside world, so can learn more quickly than Celie if we listen to that inner voice and take action.

You are a powerful person. Stand in your strength. You'll be amazed at how much you will accomplish when you know you are strong.

Spirit, we know that you are with us every moment guiding our actions and protecting us from harm. We know that you created us to be powerful people. Because we know this in our brains, we now claim this power for our souls, our actions, and our futures.

PREPARE FOR YOUR DREAMS

"Follow your dreams to reach your goals, and follow your goals to reach your dreams." -Pamela Harper

Harper continued by saying, "When you know what you really want out of life, your dreams align with daily goals. Great relationships don't just happen; they are part of a grand plan. Winners dream big and travel far."

What she is telling us is that when our dreams, our goals, and our daily actions are aligned, we will see success. We cannot fulfill our dreams if one of those components is missing or out of alignment.

For example, many of us would like to win the lottery and share our winnings with our families, making life easier for all. But, and this is a big "BUT," if we don't buy lottery tickets, then not having a ticket makes reaching our goals and dreams impossible. Not buying tickets prevents us from winning the multi-million-dollar jackpot. This is a simple example, so let's explore something more difficult:

Let's suppose that at work the Human Resources department posts a notice that the company is hiring for the job we've wanted a long time. We had prepared for the opportunity by taking career development courses and showing initiative on our projects. Finally, that special job is available. We rush to update our resumes and submit them well before the due date.

As we wait for the interview process, we begin watching our coworkers. This one dresses more professionally then we do. That one has a master's degree in our chosen field. We have more years of experience, but what is that compared to MS degrees and professional wardrobes? Our hair is starting to turn gray. Who would hire an old person for this dynamic position?

Do you see what is happening? We prepared for the opportunity. We followed the application process. Then we began doubting that the managers would hire someone like us. We just talked ourselves out of our dream job. Many of us do this every day.

Some of us don't even have dreams and goals. How can we reach our dream if we don't know what it is? Growing up with parents who lived through the Great Depression taught many of us that we should be happy just to have a job and pay the bills. We never allowed ourselves to dream. If we don't have dreams, how can we set goals? If we don't have goals, how can we prepare ourselves for the big opportunity? If we aren't prepared, we won't be hired.

It's not too late to dream and set goals, no matter what our age. Some people have earned their degrees after retirement, even in their 80s and 90s. (My mother graduated high school at age 52. She attended classes for three years to reach her goal and live her dream.)

So here we are, some of us with gray hair or no hair, and we've finally realized that underneath "real life" we always had a dream to be this or that. We need to make a list of what training is necessary and set a goal to prepare ourselves for the opportunity, should it arise. We should take whatever training is necessary. Sometimes being self-taught is just as good as a degree. All the while, in our minds' eyes, we should envision ourselves reaching that goal. Inside we should feel what the experience will be.

Feeling is the missing piece. We need to feel our dream in our minds and in our bodies. Our whole being must be aligned to that one goal. No matter what else is happening in our lives, we need to do one small thing each day that will move us closer to our goals.

Spirit, we thank you this day for reminding us that we are never too old, or too anything, to live our dream. We acknowledge all the barriers that stand in our way. We choose to receive your help in setting and reaching our goals. We choose to ask you to help us stay focused on those goals and not give up when people make negative comments or when impediments stand in our way. We trust that all will fall into place, and our dreams will come true.

EMBRACE CHANGE

"... the only way to find permanent joy is by embracing the fact that nothing is permanent." -Martha Beck*

Non-permanence is a hard concept to grasp. From the time we were very small, we were taught the difference between permanent and temporary. Our parents taught us that candy is temporary, but that they would never leave us. When we started first grade, they told us that our baby teeth would fall out and would be replaced by permanent teeth. Then teachers told us to behave, or our misbehavior would go on our permanent record.

As we matured we learned that candy might be temporary and also that "a moment on the lips is forever on the hips" is true. Eventually, either we chose to leave home, or our parents left us by disagreement or by death. Our baby teeth fell out. Some permanent teeth may have disappeared too. We learned that our childhood misdemeanors didn't follow us into the work world.

We learned that many things that we thought were forever, weren't, like friends, marriages, good jobs and on and on. We learned that "happily ever after" was a myth, but on the bright side, so was "sadly ever after." An example of a difficult lesson learned is when I once worked with a woman who frustrated me. Whenever I complained about something, she nodded and said, "This too shall pass." When I bragged that something wonderful had happened, she smiled and said, "This too shall pass." Eventually, her lesson that nothing is permanent began to sink into my belief system.

The world has evolved dramatically. We may not feel comfortable with the rapid changes. Our old ideas about how things work no longer apply. I wonder if I have shifted my belief system enough to keep up with all those changes. All I can do is try to keep current. However, the biggest change I see is a personal one. I think differently about life, God, and myself now. For example, I see myself as a nice person, the type who is kind to puppies and understanding of another person's foibles. Yet I know I could do better, so I'll continuing looking for change.

Other people can't change me. Only I can work that miracle. Good intentions won't do the job. I wish I could say, "From now on, I'll be kind to every person I meet no matter how they act or what they say," and that would be my action, but that's not possible. What I can do is determine that I want to redefine who I am and watch it happen a little each day.

Spirit, thank you for showing us that nothing is permanent, whether it be painful or joyous. We know that even the oceans and the mountains change over time, and so must we. Change can be painful or easy and joyful. Either way, the change will be for the better if we allow it to happen in its own way.

*Beck, Martha, "Daily Inspiration," info@marthabeck.com, March 9, 2016

AGE PROVIDES LESSONS

"The hardest years in life are those between 10 and 70." - Helen Hayes*

That is, indeed, good news, something I needed to hear on this dark, cold February morning! A few days ago I turned 70, the culmination of a 69-year roller-coaster ride. The past several weeks have been a period of reflection, looking at good times and bad and realizing that they were all just experiences that made me who I am today.

While birthdays brought just a continuation of the year before, decades were a little different. For instance, on my 20th birthday I was married, expecting a baby and looking forward to turning 21 so I could vote. By the time my 40th came along, my children had all left home. I was single and starting to think about attending college. Then one day I was 60, and life had changed dramatically. I was retired but still working and living near my daughters, their husbands, and my almost adult grandchildren.

Now, at 70, a new chapter is beginning. I'm not sure what that means. I'm still working, enjoying play dates with four great-grandsons, and still hoping to write the great American novel. While my current job cushions the limitations of Social Security income, more importantly, it provides valuable social interaction and is FUN.

When I was younger, a job was something I survived eight hours a day to feed the children and later myself. Age brings knowledge that I was the source of most of my discontent of that time period. I was much too concerned with what others thought of me; well, what I believed they thought of me is a more accurate statement.

Another thing I've learned is that I now have something important to say, and I'm saying it in my blogs. I've also learned that there are times and places to keep my thoughts to myself. I allow my daughters to take care of me in little ways. They go to doctor appointments with me to take notes and ask questions that I forget. They advise me about this and that and check to be sure my refrigerator is full. Rather than considering that nosiness, I look at it as caring that I'm eating properly.

Who knows what this decade will bring? From this view point, I foresee many more play dates with the great-grandsons, continuing to work at a fun job, and riding my bicycle around the neighborhood. I don't have the strength and energy that I used to have, and I miss those. But the lack of strength and energy has been replaced by a life-view that is more patient with my shortcomings and those of others.

What other people do is not so important anymore. How I spend my days is much more important. Did I do something fun today? Did I feel grateful? Did I think kind thoughts about someone? Did I eat something just because it tastes good? Did I take a nap because I wanted to? Did I do something useful?

Spirit, thank you for seventy years of learning and for more years to enjoy what I've learned. Thank you for being patient while I struggled to understand what is important. Thank you for a future to practice what has taken me so long to learn!

*Hayes, Helen, from *Treasury of Women's Quotations* by Carolyn Warner, Prentiss Hall

SMALL STEPS

"I don't look to jump over seven-foot bars. I look around for one-foot bars that I can step over." -Warren Buffet

What a lot of wisdom in two short sentences! Most of us set our goals too high, which sets the scene for failure. Then we whine, "Nothing works out for me. Everything I try fails." Is that really true? Or, are we so focused on the big picture that we fail to see our small victories along the way? Let's look at this a little closer.

One example to which many of us can relate is that of my friend whose doctor told her to lose 100 pounds in a year. She fell apart when she heard that. "One hundred pounds!" she cried. "How will I ever do that?" Like many of us, she has lost and regained 10 pounds here and 20 pounds there several times over the years, easily varying 100 pounds or more.

Fortunately, my friend's health plan offers a sensible weight loss program that is guiding her step by step along the way. She also joined TOPS (Take Off Pounds Sensibly). Her companions in that group celebrate each pound or half-pound that she sheds.

My friend has also changed her vocabulary. A wise woman said, "When you say you've lost 10 pounds, your body thinks you've lost something you need and goes looking for a way to find it again." She suggested saying, "I shed unnecessary weight." That way your body feels good for helping you stay healthy. Additionally, my friend no longer says things like, "I can't eat that cake." Instead she says, "I choose not to eat cake today."

All this is a long way of saying that each time my friend chooses not to eat cake, she is stepping over a one-foot-bar. When she was thinking, "100 pounds!" she was seeing a seven-foot-bar, an impossible leap. By stepping over several one-foot-bars, she will reach the goal recommended by her doctor, and she will do it in a healthy way that will not set her up for future failure.

Of course, this weight loss example is not the only way we set ourselves up for failure by attempting that seven-foot-bar. This lesson can also apply to learning a new language, saving money for college, finding a new job that pays double the old salary, redecorating the house, or becoming enlightened. All are seven-foot-bars until we realize that the successful path is not a straight and narrow road to victory; rather, our path is strewn with zigs and zags and several one-foot-bars requiring us to lift our eyes and our feet just a little higher than they were a moment before. Each small obstacle overcome puts us closer to our goal, if we choose to see it that way.

Spirit, we will face many obstacles as we walk our path to physical, mental, emotional and spiritual health. We know that we can climb every hill or jump every puddle as long as we see these as small, rather than impossible, obstacles. We choose today to perceive these problems as a stairway to success to whatever our goal. We know this is true, because you have promised it. We claim it.

BELIEVE IN YOURSELF

"Argue for your limitations, and sure enough, they're yours." - Richard Bach

As children we were taught to be modest, a valuable trait. However, many of us took that to mean that we should always understate what we do and what we have. That thought pattern becomes our personal belief and is reflected in our actions.

We say such things as, "Thank you, but rescuing that puppy from a burning house was nothing. Anyone would do it and do it better than I." This attitude shows up in our professional lives when our supervisor says, "Can you do this project?" and we respond, "I'll try." Then when the boss selects someone else for the project, we say, "I could do a better job than that person," and we suffer from hurt feelings. We chalk this up as another failure to our list of personal disasters.

The problem with this kind of thinking and speaking is that not only do our supervisors and coworkers think we are incompetent, so do we. We may know that we have the skills required, but we are not sure if we can implement the project. This is not a good way to earn promotions, nor to win friends and influence people! Often our modesty training has been with us so long that we truly believe we are "less than, not as smart as, not as beautiful as" and other demeaning comparisons.

Let's adopt Muhammed Ali's "I am the greatest" philosophy. It's true! Someone once said, "God don't make no junk." That applies to every one of us.

We don't walk around proclaiming those words aloud to others, but it doesn't do any harm to say "I am the greatest!" to ourselves each day until we believe it. Do you think that Ali would have been champion if he didn't believe he was the greatest?

Let's walk the walk and talk the talk in a quiet way. Eventually we will know in our hearts that we can do whatever is required of us. Our personal talent will begin to show and glow. Once we know that we can do it, whatever "it" is, so will other people.

God, thank you for this new day and the awareness you have given us. Each of us has a special talent, even though we don't always see it. Remind us each day that you made us for a purpose and what that purpose is. Give us glimpses that remind us that we are the greatest. Let each of those glimpses grow in our hearts until we truly believe it to be so.

DO IT ANYWAY

"You gain strength, courage and confidence by every experience in which you really stop to look fear in the face. You must do the thing which you think you cannot do." - Eleanor Roosevelt

We all have fears, even those of us who think we are fearless. Some of us are afraid of spiders, flying, and loud noises. Others fear the dark, being alone, and making a mistake. Each day, no matter how we try to plan our lives so we don't encounter our fears, we face them anyway.

Many times our fears protect us from danger. We know that if we go swimming during a hurricane we will drown. If we play golf in a thunderstorm, we have a good chance of being struck by lightning. Those fears are based on facts and have been proven many times. So our reactions to these events isn't fear. No, we are acting on knowledge (or what our parents called common sense).

Often we allow our fears to control our lives by avoiding confrontations, high places, or anything that intimidates us. Usually our fears are based on previous experiences, especially fears of speaking up or challenging another's statements. But if we avoid these situations, we live limited lives. It is only by standing up for our beliefs that we become the people we were meant to be. We were not put on this Earth to cower but to live fully.

In the quote at the top of this page, Mrs. Roosevelt states so clearly why we must face our fears. Only by doing "the thing which you think you cannot do" can we grow to be better people than we were yesterday. Sometimes we have to face a situation many times before we can do it confidently.

Facing fear is like taking our turn at bat in a baseball game. Initially, we learn to face the ball and not duck when we see it coming toward us. Then we get brave enough to swing the bat, and we feel warm inside. Then we hit the ball, and even though it doesn't go far, we think we might learn how to play the game, after all. Slowly we learn how to take a stance, how to hold the bat, and how to swing. Finally, one day we step up to the plate, take a mighty swing, and hit a home run. We did it!

As we become more confident in our own abilities, whether at home plate or on the job, so do others become confident in us. We find that we are earning their respect. Our friends begin to ask for our advice; whereas, previously, we asked them to tell us what to do. Doing what needs to be done makes us a better person, someone we are proud to be. Learning to live up to our full potential is why we were put on this earth.

Creator spirit, thank you for teaching us that we learn by doing. Each attempt at a new skill gives us more confidence to do that thing and do it well. Facing fear is just another new skill we need to learn. Confidence doesn't come easily. We have to learn and earn it. We thank you for presenting opportunities to grow into the people you want us to be. We thank you for the warm feeling you give us each time we succeed in a new skill, whether the skill is mechanical or psychological.

WHO AM I?

"What should I be but just what I am?" -Edna St. Vincent Millay*

This quote says everything about us. Yet we don't believe it. Most of us spend too much time finding fault with what we were given or have accumulated. We think:

I weigh too much.

I don't earn enough money.

I should be (insert adjective or noun here.)

And on and on and on.

On one level, I believe that I am just what I am supposed to be. Yet I find it hard to undo the effects of people telling me for years that I'm not enough, physically, mentally and spiritually. I even have told myself these things. Often I'm learning and moving forward with what seems like amazing speed. But sometimes I feel like I'm still living in poor-me land.

So here I am, a work in progress. One day I was complaining that I wasn't "there" yet. A friend told me that we never get "there" as long as we are on this planet. We only get "there" once we've transitioned to a higher realm, whatever you choose to call it. She was right.

We're all a work in progress. We think we fall short, and often we do, because we think we are not enough. We regret that we aren't what we "should be, could be, or would be, if only...." What we need to remember is that "if only" is already inside us. We are all what we need to be. If we can accept that premise, we will move forward steadily to our destined potential. Our hopes and dreams can come true if we allow them to fulfill.

This seems impossible, and it may be. Even those we call saints found fault with themselves. However, we can accept ourselves where we are today, this minute, shortcomings and all. If we always replace a negative thought floating through our minds with the acceptance of our progress at that moment, we will see ourselves gaining on our dreams. Each step of progress we acknowledge will help us affirm that we are okay being just what we are.

Spirit, please remind us each day that we are the highest and best that we can be!

* "The Singing-Woman from the Woods", pg.38, "O, the Oprah Magazine," September, 2014

BELIEVE WHAT WE SEE

"When people show you who they are, believe them." -Dr. Maya Angelou

"I think we're so desperate to believe that we're lovable that we're gullible." -Pamela Harper

Dr. Angelou was a wise woman. From reading her books and listening to her speak, we know that she found wisdom the hard way. She told us to watch people's actions and listen to their words before deciding to have a relationship with them. The same thing applies in the work place and in our social lives. Often we ignore those signs and don't even think of them until our world has fallen apart. Then we realize that the signs were there all along.

It took me many years to learn this lesson. I committed myself to painful and demoralizing relationships. I had friends who gossiped about me behind my back while sympathizing with me to get more information. I worked at jobs that drained my confidence rather than enhance my life.

I hung on to those situations hoping that these signs were just passing episodes. I believed that those men I loved would change their stripes and become supportive, loving partners. I believed my friends really cared about my well-being. I believed that if I just worked a little harder, the job would be the right fit.

Eventually, I learned that those people and situations were who and what they were and would not change. Even worse, I learned the signs had been there in the beginning, before I even made the commitment to them. That realization demoralized me until I realized that I had suffered long enough and decided to change my way of looking at the world.

I became more aware of subtleties in various situations and discussions I was involved in – not suspicious, but aware. I still look for the best in people and situations, but I keep my eyes open for signs of disrespect. By being aware and learning to step away from potentially hurtful situations, I have come to respect myself and my judgment.

What a wonderful lesson! I learned that I am not a hopeless klutz who keeps falling into bad situations, but a wise woman capable of making intelligent decisions. The result: fewer negative people and events are in my life, and many enriching experiences and loving persons abound in it.

Spirit, thank you for giving each of us the wisdom to see what is before our eyes, to recognize the signs of approaching danger, and to make decisions that will enhance our lives rather than damage them!

LOVE IS SELF-APPROVAL

"Ultimately, love is self-approval" -Sondra Ray

"It is very easy to forgive others their mistakes; it takes more grit and gumption to forgive them for having witnessed your own." -Jessamyn West

Sometimes we just can't see how much we've grown or know if we are still stuck in our self-pity, self-anger, or self-flagellation. Sometimes we have to be confronted by dear friends who are tired of hearing us say, "I'm fine," when they know that we're not. They challenge our statements that we're no longer stuck in our old ruts when they can plainly see that we've only crawled part way out.

Our friends say, "I don't believe you. You are deceiving yourself. You don't do such and such as much as you used to, but you still do it." When they say this, we cry, not only because we haven't grown as much as we thought, but also because we have disappointed our friends.

Suddenly, we remember something we did just because we wanted to, and we tell our friends about it. They ask, "Did you do that because you wanted to, or because you thought it was something you should do?"

"Because I wanted to."

"Really?"

"Yes."

Hugs follow, along with congratulations for finally doing something for myself. That confirmation gives me the courage to say that the next day I will be seeing my former husband and his family. My friends ask if I want to see them. I respond that I want to see the family, but I am not sure about seeing my former husband. They tell me to think about it before the actual event.

I did. The next day, I took extra care with my dress and makeup and realized I was looking forward to the visit. When I arrived everyone was laughing and having a great time. Previous visits had felt tense. I was greeted with hugs and love, and soon I was laughing with everyone else. The love and joy lasted throughout the visit. I wasn't sure why until I read the second quote at the beginning of this message. While I had let go of our mutual bad behaviors, I couldn't let go of the knowledge that my ex-husband had witnessed me at my worst. Somehow, by beginning to do things for my own pleasure, I was able to let go of that unpleasant knowledge and fears that confined me.

Freedom at last!

Spirit, we thank you for freedom from fear, self-loathing, and any other thoughts that keep us from being the best people we can be. You have promised that we can be more than we can see with our limited vision. We tend to keep our eyes and ears closed until that moment when we must face the truth of our existence. But once we realize that your promises are real and accept them, we can live in freedom and offer peace, love and joy to all we encounter.

CHOOSE TO BE BRAVE

"Should you ever find yourself on your path moving along in spite of fear, wondering if you're ready or not to rise to the next level, chances are great that you will not be ready. Rise anyway. You see, wondering means you're not ready, doing means you are." - Mike Dooley*

Some people seem to be always ready to walk a new path, apply for a new job, or dive off the high board. Others seem to be afraid to try anything new. Most of us are somewhere in the middle. We're eager to try new things as long as the risk isn't too scary, but we shy away from life-changing possibilities.

I wander up and down the readiness ladder.

Once I tried for a job that sounded fun just for the application experience, knowing I wouldn't be hired. Even though my skill set wasn't exactly what they had in mind, I was hired because I'd done a number of different jobs and showed that I adapt easily to change. That job turned out to be my favorite. It felt more like fun than work.

I've moved to different states without a lot of thought. Sometimes those moves were beneficial and made me happy. Others were dead ends that made me want to flee within the first hour, if I could have. It never was possible, and I learned valuable lessons from those choices.

Then there are smaller risks, like riding roller coasters. I've always been the one waiting on the ground for my friends to descend from their heart-racing adventure. Recently, the doctor told me to stay off roller coasters. Relief! Now I have a valid excuse to stay on the ground.

Writing my blog, "Thoughts to Ponder," was frightening at first. Who was I to offer life suggestions to others who probably knew more than I? However, I've learned that most people enjoy reading the blogs, and they thank me for presenting a new idea. Those who don't agree with what I write usually don't comment.

Now folks are urging me to write a book. That is a terrifying thought! How can I stretch 500-800-word ponderings into a 50-

80,000-word book of these? Who would edit it? Who would publish it? Who would buy it and read it? At this point (the time of this writing), I'm still considering those questions. Recently, I wrote about a meditation in which I was directed to step off a cliff. As soon as I can determine how to turn 500 words into 60,000, I'll take that step, knowing other issues will be resolved as I write.

In the meantime, I hope that, like me, you will take a little risk, then a larger one, and then step off the cliff. You just might find a wonderful adventure.

*Mike Dooley, A Note from the Universe, February 17, 2015, www.tut.com

HEALING WOUNDS

"The more we try to keep our wounds concealed, the more they will emerge into the areas of our life that do not pertain to our wound." -Window of Wisdom 985*

That single sentence says in a few words what takes most of us years of talk therapy, 12-step meetings, and journaling to understand. Some of us just go about our business hoping no one guesses what we have endured or cope with in our daily lives. We think our bravado and competence erase all traces of pain, but we're wrong. It slips out in little ways.

We may lose our tempers when a situation really doesn't warrant that reaction. We may accuse a person of being an alcoholic, thief, or a slacker. We may demand punctuality without excuse, reasonable or not.

We may laugh too much at jokes or maintain a jolly demeanor. We may overly dramatize an unpleasant situation when relating the story to others. We might act like a hurtful event had no impact.

We've all experienced wounds and have learned to cope in various ways. The most effective way that I've found, and this is recommended by most therapists, is to feel the pain in the moment, even if the hurt was caused by something as simple as a rude word. Take whatever time necessary to feel the feelings, but don't wallow in them. Continue going to work and follow your regular schedule as much as possible. Don't use being hurt as an excuse to fail; and don't try to numb the pain by overcompensating.

Here is one example. My father, who had lived the horrors of Alzheimer's Disease for many years, transitioned three days before his birthday in December, 1993. I had watched him slide from a strong, humorous man to a frail skeleton of a man lying in a nursing home. When he died, I was so relieved that he was out of his misery that I had little reaction to his leaving Earth. When anyone asked, I said, "He's out of pain and confusion now. I'm glad he's in a better place."

In May, 2010, my mother, who had lived with the discomfort of colon cancer and had chosen not to treat it, departed the Earthly plane. Again, I was relieved that she was out of pain and her own personal sadness. After a few tears, I took affairs in hand and did what had to be done. Soon after returning home, I called work and said I was ready to return. My supervisor questioned that decision, but I insisted that all was well.

The next year, my son passed of a heart attack on the anniversary of his grandfather's funeral. I took the news fairly calmly to not upset his partner, who was still grieving the loss of her son. But after hanging up the phone, I descended into hysterics. Fortunately, a friend came to my rescue. She told me to breathe, breathe again, and yet again. When I became somewhat coherent, she told me how to notify his sisters, and she gave me each thing I had to do to prepare for the three-day drive to Minnesota to handle his affairs. As I began to pull myself together, I put my pain in a safe place and soldiered on. Soon I was back at work and participating in all my normal activities.

The following December, the grief of all three losses hit me like a brick. I was working at a place where Christmas is the busiest, happiest time of year. Fortunately, I'd learned a little about myself and how to deal with life. I told my supervisor what was happening and that I was going to allow myself to feel my feelings while, at the same time, I would try to be a pleasant helper to our guests. He, of course, kept a close eye on me.

After Christmas our business closed to prepare for the next season. I had time off. That gave me time to allow the feelings about all three passings to flood over me. If I felt like crying, I cried. If I felt like swearing at them for abandoning me, I swore. If I felt like talking about them as if they were saints, I did that. By the time work resumed, I was ready to go back. I had done what I needed to do to heal myself.

I realize not everyone has the gift of a three-month quiet time to heal their wounds. However, everyone has a few minutes each day to feel their feelings. They can honestly evaluate where they are in the process of healing pain, dealing with an angry situation, or just slogging through daily burdens. Taking this time is the key to healing. It is a vital step. It sets the tone for the rest of their lives. We can say, "It's all behind us," but only this quiet time will tell us the truth.

Beyond healing our pain, there is another upside to surviving personal devastation. It's called Post-Traumatic Growth (PTG). ** "Growth results from an active, engaged process of dealing with a stressor – not the stressor itself." ***

This occurs when we have accepted and learned to live with our personal disasters. For example: From my dad, I learned to be sad, angry and fearful when I'm with a safe friend. The rest of the time, I can look at life's foibles with a sense of humor. My mom taught me, in a backwards way, that it's okay to feel sad, but not to let sadness dominate my days and years. I learned from my son to be more adventuresome and willing to try new experiences. What gifts they've given me!

Spirit, thank you for this opportunity to heal everything and anything that weighs us down. We know that releasing our pain is the only way to heal. We know that we will continue to have periods of sadness, but, because we have done the healing work, we need not worry that the pain tumor will burst at an inopportune time.

*"A Window of Wisdom," December 14, 2015, https://awindowofwisdom.wordpress.com/2015/12/14/window-985-stop-suffering-and -release-the-pain

** "Is There an Upside to Tragedy?", Ginny Graves, quoting Richard Tedeschi, PhD, University of North Carolina-Charlotte and Lawrence Calhoun, PhD., "O the Oprah Magazine," July, 2015

*** Suzanne, Danhauser, PhD, Wake Forest School of Medicine, "Is There an Upside to Tragedy?", "O the Oprah Magazine," July 2015

FINDING YOUR WAY

"Don't worry about losing your way. If you do, pain will remind you to find your path again. Joy will let you know when you are back on it." -Martha Beck*

We all feel lost at some time in our lives. Even those who appear to have their lives in perfect order have felt lost but have found their way back to their true path. Some are fortunate to know their future goal from the time they are children and follow the path that will take them there. Others found their path as young adults. Some of us find our path late in life after stumbling around and banging our heads into trees that stand in our way.

As Beck says, "pain will remind you to find your path again." I've felt that pain over and over, not knowing what direction I should be travelling. That's not to say that each path has been a disaster. On the contrary, each path has given me gifts and taught me valuable lessons. One path led to three beautiful children who grew to be fantastic adults. Another path taught me about inter-racial relations. One taught me the futility of holding on to toxic hope. The list continues. Often I tried to force my life down two or three paths at once. Talk about confusion!

If we follow our inner guidance, we reach the day when Beck says, "Joy will let you know when you are back on it." What a gift to know that we are spending our days as we should! A feeling of peace and joy will fill our hours rather than fear and dread.

Some days I still feel bogged down, but I find that I've just reached a huge mud-puddle in the middle of my path. I have learned, but don't always remember right away, to look around and see what steps I can take to avoid the mess. I give thanks to Spirit that when this happens and I feel confused, a prompting tells me, "Hey look over here! There's a plank crossing the mud puddle. You can walk on that rather than slogging through that mess."

Our life does not come with a guarantee for happiness. Even those we envy have days, weeks, or years of heartbreak and challenges. We can learn to discern whether what we are facing is an obstacle we should avoid or if it is a situation that will lead us to a better way of living. By being quiet and listening to guidance, by paying attention to the underlying messages in our dreams, and by just listening to others, we learn whether we are on the correct path or if we need to look for another route.

*Daily Inspiration, April 29, 2015, from "Leaving the Saints," Martha Beck, Inc.

Chapter Six: Awareness

DON'T WORRY ABOUT....

"By surrendering the 'cursed hows' (as in how your dreams will come true) to life's magic, you not only free yourself up to imagine your dreams without fear, but you free me up to bring about those dreams much faster (as in double-pronto, zippy). Fear not, and fasten your seat belt, because sweet change can come so fast." -The Universe (Mike Dooley)

We are an analytical people. We have to examine every action in our lives. How did that happen? Or, even worse, how will that happen?

In certain instances, analysis is required, such as constructing a building or doing surgery. Those and many other tasks require careful evaluation and planning before we can begin. Even so, we know that situations arise, and we must simply act according to the situation. We cannot plan for every contingency.

Much of our lives are based on trust and hope. We don't know, or need to know, the how of every situation. By planning all the hows, we limit the Universe's ability to help us. An old saying goes, "If you want to make God laugh, tell him your plans." May I give you a couple examples from my own life?

From middle school on, I had a goal to get a college degree. But I thought I needed to take this action and that step and to have a certain amount of money in the bank in order to go there after high school graduation. Life didn't turn out that way. Many years later, after my children left home, I decided that if I was going to attend college, now was the time.

I prayed, "God, you know I want to go to college and that I have no saved money. I'm going to enroll. I trust you will provide the tuition if you want me to go." I did this each semester, not thinking about the following semester. Every semester the money was there. Some came from fellowships and some from student loans. I was so focused on each current semester that I was shocked when I received the notice that it was time to make graduation plans. A huge blessing for me was that I graduated with less debt than many of my classmates.

All of this happened because I didn't ask how I would pay for college or how I would work full-time and get my homework done. I said my prayers and trusted God.

Another example is when I bought my house. I retired early, moved to Williamsburg, and moved into low-income housing. I was not happy there, so I told God that I wanted my own house, and I had no idea how that would happen. I said that I wanted trees, a lot of windows, one-story, and a mixed-generation, mixed-ethnic neighborhood. Soon someone told me about a program for low-income, first-time home buyers. I enrolled, took its classes, and completed the paperwork. Before long, I was approved to buy a home. I contacted a realtor and told her what I wanted and what price I had been approved to pay by the program.

Shortly, she called and said she had three houses for me to view. We scheduled a time, and I asked my daughters to go along. I didn't want to make such a big decision on my own. When we met the realtor told me that one house was sold and another owner was out of town, leaving just one house to view. When we arrived at the house, my daughters walked in first. They turned to me and said, "Mom, this is your house." Once I walked through the door, I agreed. It was perfect for me. The owner accepted my bid, and I became a home owner.

I'm completely convinced that these events occurred because I did not worry about how they would happen or how I would pay. When I remember to turn the "how" over to Spirit, good things happen. When I insist that things occur in a certain way, the situation does not work out in my favor.

Spirit, thank you for these examples of how things work in our Universe. We know what we want, but we can't figure out how we can make them happen. We are learning that if we state our desires and let you take care of the "how," life flows more smoothly. We can spend more time smiling when we let go of the "how." Thank you for this lesson.

LISTEN AND ACT

"If you can hear differences between the voices of your heart and mind, you are not insane… you are awakening." -Window of Wisdom*

How many times have we been told that people who hear voices or talk to themselves are crazy? I'm occasionally reminded, "You're talking to yourself again." My usual response is, "I'm the best conversationalist I know." To me, talking to myself is just a verbal method of solving a problem. When I try to think out a problem, my thoughts go round in circles.

I also draw maps in the air when I can take multiple routes to arrive at my desired location. I could draw the maps on paper, but I don't usually have any in the car. My mother used to think that was the silliest thing she'd ever seen, but I always managed deliver us to our destination without any problem. These traits just mean that I'm a verbal and visual thinker.

All this is just a long way to get to our topic about thinking with our hearts instead of our minds. Most scientists tell us we have one method of thinking – our brains. Our brains are so amazing. I doubt that technology will ever build a computer that can think the way humans do. They only know what we program into them from our brains.

Our brains can tell us how to build a bridge or how to spell words, but they can't tell us if the bridge should be built. Only our hearts, or consciousness if you prefer, can tell us that. The computer may tell us that if we build the bridge, we will need to dig out the natural embankment and possibly kill a unique species that lives there. Only our inner guidance can tell us if our world will be better off with or without that species.

On a more personal level, we can think that our friend just said something rude. But only our hearts can tell us if we should rebuke our friend or apologize to the person who received the rude comment. We need to decide if we want to hurt our friend's feelings or the other person's. Only our inner self can decide if we want to continue being friends with a rude person.

Every day we receive pleas for donations in the mail. This one will feed poor people. That one will save 100 acres of green space. Another will provide habitat for an endangered species. All are worthy causes. Our brain can calculate how much money we have and what amount is already designated for bills, school clothes and donations. We know that we must meet our obligations. What we need to decide is where to most effectively spend our charity funds. That is a heart decision. What cause touches us most deeply?

The quote says, "If you can hear differences between the voices of your heart and mind, you are not insane… you are awakening." That means that when we become aware that not all thoughts are logical and that some come from a deeper part of us, we are becoming aware of our ability to change the world with our words and actions. We were designed to feel as well as think. Each incident that brings us closer to our feeling center brings us closer to reaching our full potential.

Spirit, thank you for making us aware of the still voice inside that guides us to do the right thing and for giving us the courage to follow that advice.

* "A Window of Wisdom," #887, September 7, 2015

STAY IN THE MOMENT

"There is no vacation from reality, but when we strive to remain present in every moment, a vacation becomes a part of our reality, instead of an escape." - A Window of Wisdom*

This interesting quote not only discusses being present, but it also brings up the concept of reality. Let's talk about being present first.

"Remain present and live in the moment" were strange words to me when I first heard them. I couldn't imagine a life without my brain bouncing forward to worries and backward to hurts or regrets. That was simply the way it functioned. How I ever got any real-time work accomplished is a mystery. In addition to not working up to my abilities, my vocabulary was filled with buts and ifs. It's no wonder that what my teachers wrote on my report cards, "Doesn't work up to potential," was replicated year after year on my performance reviews!

After hearing "Live in the present" more times than I could count, I decided it might be worth a try. At first I struggled and had to constantly remind myself that I was here, today, in this place and not in whatever time and place was filling my thoughts. Sometime later, I moved from struggling to striving. Striving was easier. It was a goal I set myself each day, and I still do.

For the most part, I now live in the moment or at least in the day. When I find myself focused on events of the past or possibilities of the future, I remind myself that I am here, today, in this moment, and I bring my thoughts back to the moment. That allows me to be fully aware and to function on a higher level. A bonus of this focusing is that my performance reviews have improved significantly. I still keep a schedule, but now it is a guideline, not an "OMG, how will I get all this done?" list.

The writer's phrase, "… a vacation becomes a part of our reality, instead of an escape," struck me as strange until I realized that vacations are now a treat, not an escape. I still count down the days to my upcoming adventure, but my perspective is different. I no longer think, "Only ten more days and I'll be out of here for a week." What a difference this has made to my attitude and my work ethic! This isn't to say I never get tired and look forward to a break. I do, but the thought process makes all the difference.

Just a quick note about reality: Reality is a concept, a personal construction. Just because I experience an event a certain way doesn't mean that my experience is the only one. Each of us has a different perception of what happens. This is enough on that topic, for today anyway.

This has been a long month without writing. Regrettably, I spent most of that time slogging through the worst head cold I've had in years. My sinuses were so stuffy that my brain didn't have room to function. My thoughts centered on only one question: Will I have time to reach for another tissue before the next sneeze comes? That certainly kept me in the present. Thankfully, the cold has passed, and I'm now functioning as I should and glad to be back at the keyboard.

*Window of Wisdom 704 – "The prison of our mind," https://awindowofwisdom.wordpress.com

"Listen to your heart. It knows all things, because it came from the Soul of the World, and it will one day return there." -The Alchemist*

Listening to our hearts is often difficult. Some people do it instinctively. Regrettably, most of us tend to listen to outside voices, rather than to our hearts and bodies.

Just watch a newborn, and you will see that he knows what he needs. She cries when she is hungry and automatically turns to her mother's breast. He cries when he is wet, and we respond by changing his diaper. Of course, we've all experienced times when neither the bottle nor the diaper meet the baby's needs, and we pace the floor for hours trying to soothe her. The baby knows what he needs, but we are thinking in adult mode, so are unable to provide it.

As we grow we are taught to conform to expected norms. We sit still in school, do our homework, then sit in front of the television because our parents fear what lies outside. I'm not saying that the fear is unreasonable. It just doesn't fit what our bodies and hearts need.

We continue to grow along these patterns and follow anticipated social norms. Then one day we are adults who don't know what we want to do. We just know that what we are doing doesn't feel right. We are unhappy and make those around us unhappy. Too many souls return to the Universe with sad hearts.

Some of us rebel and are considered learning-disabled or socially unacceptable. Many people who contribute scientific discoveries or beauty to our world were once slotted into that category.

Some of us don't comprehend our path until we are older and have to dig down into our souls to find the courage to follow our hearts. The change can be difficult but rewarding as old worries, heavy hearts, and body pains fade away, and we begin to follow our new, but original, paths.

A few of us are fortunate to understand our calling while still children and are encouraged by those around us to follow our hearts. What a joy to live that life!

If we as adults can learn to follow our hearts, we will raise a whole generation of children who live according to their hearts. Can you imagine how wonderful that will be?

Spirit, please open our souls to hear our hearts calling. We know they never stopped calling. We stopped listening. We choose to live according to our heart-knowledge, realizing that we and everyone around us will be happier. We choose to return to the Universe with happy hearts.

The Alchemist by Paulo Coehlo, pg. 132, HarperCollins Publishers

"Today, give love and comfort to the starving pup inside you. Then let the love and comfort guide any action you take. It's a simple little practice. It might not save the world. But then again, it might." -Martha Beck*

We all have an inner pup even if we don't think so. Most of us deny its existence and starve the poor thing, thinking that the persona we portray to others is the real us.

Some of us were fortunate to be nurtured by family and friends, allowing our inner pup to grow to be a strong, healthy dog as we grew to maturity. Those inner dogs learned to love and protect us.

Often something terrible happened along the way that caused us put the young dog in a pen. These are the animals that tend to bite or at least snarl at perceived attackers. We reflect those behaviors when we feel threatened.

Others of us were never allowed to let our pup grow. Perhaps the causes were verbal or physical brutality or unreasonably high expectations. "You will be an A+ student, outstanding athlete, and succeed in business, thus bringing honor to your family." These actions and unmet expectations kept our pup in its training cage so it could not run and play as it grew. Since our pup couldn't mature, neither could we.

My family believed that dreams were for others. Our job was to grow strong, work hard, have a little fun, and, if we were lucky, die peacefully without pain. Low expectations can also hinder the pup, just as unreasonably high expectations can.

Even though my parents were proud of my making the honor roll, they seldom mentioned it because it might make others feel badly if their children didn't do the same. When I reached middle school and teachers began suggesting that I prepare for college, I was told that college was for rich people. I was also told that the professors would teach me useless information and erase my common sense.

Somehow my inner pup told me that I had to leave the area of my home if I wanted to fulfill my dreams, whatever they were. I'd never allowed myself to envision or verbalize a dream. That led me to accept a marriage proposal from a military man. Whatever happened, I'd get to see some of the world. I had three fantastic children, met some wonderful people, and lived in places I'd never imagined. Even with all those gifts, one day my inner pup told me to leave my marriage. I did, and I experienced life's ups and downs over the next several years.

One of those gifts came the day I read an article about area colleges, and my pup began barking like crazy. Even though I had no savings and could barely meet my bills, I listened to the pup's advice and enrolled at Alverno College in Milwaukee. I graduated five years later with less student debt than most of my classmates. My pup had even found some grants and fellowship dollars. That education led me to some good jobs that were also fun. Those that weren't so good were the jobs I had sought simply for higher wages.

As I approached age 55 my inner pup began barking again, leading me to retire early so that I could live near my children and grandchildren in Virginia. She told me that if I waited until full retirement age, my grandchildren would be adults and strangers to me. I took the leap and became friends with my sons-in-law and grandchildren. Now I have four great-grandsons who are the light of my heart.

Even with all her good advice, I still tend to push my pup into her cage when I think something else is more important than what she has to say. Sometimes I listen to her. While sitting at the doctor's office, I allowed my pup to speak through my pen instead of reading or working a puzzle. This blog is the result.

Much of the time my inner pup is confused because my to-do list is so long. But, I've learned that *if* I listen to my furry buddy, she'll lead me in the correct direction.

*Blog article, "Loving your Inner Pup," Insight from Martha, Martha Beck Inc.

CHOOSE STILLNESS

"Your first daily priority should be stillness, attention to what you really know and what you really feel." -Martha Beck

Often we go to bed with our minds overflowing with concerns such as to-do lists, bills to pay, children's school issues, pets with fleas, and our own personal shortcomings. Our sleep is not sound and restful, so we wake up with those same thoughts racing through our minds. Not only that, but the dog needs walking. Now! Thus, the worry cycle continues for another day, interfering with our relaxation and enjoyment.

Today's quote suggests that we start the day with stillness and attention to what we know and feel. Sounds wonderful, doesn't it? But it doesn't walk the dog, fix breakfast for the family, or deal with the morning rush hour. What might happen if we take a few minutes to concentrate on stillness and attention while doing our solitary morning activities like showering or brushing our teeth?

In addition to that, imagine how soundly we could sleep if we take a few minutes to give our attention to stillness, what we know, and what we feel before we drift off to sleep? Those same thoughts will be on our minds as we awaken in the morning. They'll set the tone of the day.

Another useful tool is taking a moment to feel the inner stillness and pay attention to what is happening inside ourselves when we feel stressed or anxious. We can simply take a few deep, cleansing breaths; slow our heart beats; quiet that rumbling in our stomachs; and just be present in that moment. When we are present, our minds begin to put the brakes on the squirrel running around the wheel inside our brains. We give that squirrel a chill pill. Then we can fully comprehend the situation and make calm decisions that will lead to appropriate actions.

Spirit, we thank you for this reminder to stay calm and remain in the moment. By doing this, we will not get sucked into whatever is happening in the outside world. We can observe those events and send peace, love, and joy to all involved without taking on the weight of the situation. We know that we, and all who are around us, benefit when we are fully present and aware. In this way we can be agents of change, rather than worriers. We know this is so, because we have read it in your holy books.

WHAT IS TRUTH?

"Say not, 'I have found the truth'; but rather, 'I have found a truth.'" Kahlil Gibran

Many people say, "The truth is the truth, period." Their truth is narrow and unchangeable. Any words or actions contrary to their truth is wrong and will never be right. Sometimes their belief is so strong that they act on their truths in unusual or cruel ways.

A teacher once said, "Where you stand on an issue depends on where you sit." He meant that your life circumstances often determine what your truth will be.

Both views are clearly observable as we watch the news and talk with our neighbors. The problem is that we tend to adopt those truths because we hear them repeatedly, not because we carefully think about the possible permutations of this or that truth.

We each need to find our own truth through study, observation, and consideration of how each action or word affects us and our loved ones. Does a particular statement or action fit into our life or dreams for the future? Is it honest? Is it kind? Is it loving? Does it feel right?

Another issue is that once we find our truth, it may not be permanent. Just because an attitude was true for us when we were twenty does not necessarily mean that it is true for us at fifty. The more we observe, the more our truth changes. Our life experiences through time make us see the world with changing eyes.

Saying we've found a truth is valid. Saying we've found "the" truth is a stretch. Remember: "...Say not 'I have found the truth'; but rather, 'I have found a truth.'"

Spirit, thank you for teaching us that there is more than one side to an issue. There are even more than two. Truth is not one-size-fits-all. Each person has found or is searching for his or her truth. You've shown us that we cannot change another's point of view. We can only change ourselves by being loving, kind, and honest and by doing what feels right.

LET GO OF FALSE LIMITS

"The hurrieder I go; the behinder I get." Author unknown

Usually, I share thoughts by converting my personal experiences and lessons into "we and our" experiences. This week I had such an amazing "ah-ha" moment that I'm going to tell the story as it happened.

During the past few months, I was feeling so overwhelmed that I became sick. I've had some workers here remodeling my kitchen, both bathrooms, all my floors and my HVAC system. It had to be done. Everything was original equipment installed when the neighborhood was built in the mid-80s. As the workers completed each job, I felt so proud of the accomplishment, and I promised myself I'd do the touch-up painting "soon." I told them to leave the towel racks and wall accessories down. I would replace them after I painted.

The only fly in that stew was that the workers said that the old paint wouldn't match, and I'd have to repaint entire rooms. That meant that I would have to buy new paint and do at least three rooms before returning to work. Not only was that a lot of work and money, I was not feeling up to the task. The least amount of work wore me out. I spent most of my winter sleeping. Just call me Yogi.

A few days ago, I began rereading *The Five People You Meet in Heaven* and *Tuesdays with Morrie* by Mitch Albom. As I read I began feeling more energetic and started getting things done around the house. I even asked a friend to come and install the new toilet tissue holders because their locations did not need painting, and I was tired of knocking the rolls onto the floors. (I knew I could do the work. I'd hung rollers before, but my friend would do the job faster and neater.)

That accomplished, the next task was to hang the towel racks – in just one bathroom. The other set of racks did not need to be removed and replaced. My friend told me to do the necessary painting, and then he'd be back in two days to finish the job. I agreed and went about my evening tasks.

But yesterday morning I woke up sick and felt totally overwhelmed. I spent most of the day in my chair working on a few computer tasks. I just couldn't get the energy to start painting two bathrooms and a kitchen all in one day. I was a complete physical and mental mess. Not only was I overwhelmed by the tasks before me, I knew I'd disappoint my friend who was kind enough to offer to hang the towel racks.

Finally, bedtime arrived and I picked up my latest book, *Slow Down ... and Get More Done*, by Marshall Cook. I'd read the book years ago but had forgotten the lessons. Just looking at the cover reminded me that I didn't have to paint three rooms, including trim, for my friend to hang two towel racks. All I needed to do was paint the area where he'd be working. I could finish the rest later.

I began laughing. Immediately my overwhelmed feeling passed. I read a chapter and fell asleep. This morning I woke up early, taped the necessary borders, and then painted the pertinent area. I took a break, ate a bowl of cereal, and now I am writing this story. I'm nearly done writing, and I am willing to bet that the bathroom is ready for the second coat of paint, all before 9:30 a.m. The second coat will be dry by the time my friend arrives about noon. Then, like magic, I'll have new towel racks. I even finally decided where I want them put.

After he finishes the work, I can go back and finish the painting at a more leisurely pace. My job's new season won't start for another two weeks. That gives me plenty of time to do what needs to be done. *And* I don't need to paint the whole rooms, just the areas that were scuffed up or replaced in the remodeling. The old paint still matches.

What a difference a small thought makes! I don't have to follow the rules set by my parents and former employers. This is my project. I'm the boss and can work at my own pace. Now that the stress is lifted, I'll work more efficiently and be happier with the outcome. And I'm willing to go out on a limb and say that I'll have energy left at the end of each day.

Spirit, thank you for reminding me that time is a human construction. We impose limits on ourselves. You have given us endless time and energy. By slowing down, we get more done. By remembering what is most important, we discover that all the small tasks take care of themselves. Most of all, thank you for the gift of laughing at myself.

BE GRATEFUL

"If the only prayer you said in your life was 'thank you,' that would suffice." -Meister Eckhart

We live in a crazy world. Just days after politicians were screaming at each other and arguing over election results, they are working together to assist the people in the Philippines who have lost everything.

The typhoon is a huge event in our world, and we give it a great deal of attention. We are grateful we are here and not there. If possible, we share our cash and volunteer our time and energy to help those who have lost loved ones and homes. These acts of kindness are appreciated, and we can feel good that we helped those who have nothing. However, let's talk about everyday life:

Do we say thank you for waking to a new day?

Do we say thank you for the sun and rain?

Do we say thank you for the beauty around us?

Do we say thank you for the cold temperatures?

Do we say thank you for getting the flu?

Do we say thank you for that irascible co-worker?

You get the idea. "Gratitude" is the word of the day. Everything revolves around gratitude. Where we put our attention is what we experience. If we spend our time complaining about our incompetent co-worker, guess what we get. If we say thank you for that co-worker, we might see sparks of creativity.

If we say thank you for the flu, we might realize that we enjoyed being home and not needing to drive in the rain to get to work. We can be grateful that no one is witnessing our nasty bodily eruptions and our disgusting appearance.

Everything, no matter how awful it seems, has a gift hidden inside. An example that just came to my awareness is my son's transition. As sad as we all were, we knew that Dan went when it was his time and that he had work to do. This summer we experienced some of that work. His transition brought a healing miracle to his family.

After 40-plus years of hard feelings for all involved, our family is now united. My children's father, his wife, and their children are now friends with me and my children. We were happy to spend time together and called each other sister, cousin, brother, grandma or whatever other label fit the situation. No one used the words "step" or "half." Laughter and warm feelings ruled the two days we were together. Unpleasant events in the past were left there. They have no place in our lives today.

Thank you, Universe, God, guides, angels! The sun, moon, flowers, trees, birds, animals, friends and family, neighbors – nice or cranky - are all gifts to enjoy. All teach lessons. Illness, loss, money and lack are more gifts. We are grateful for everything we experience and look for the lessons in each event, large or small. You have promised that we will receive that which holds our attention. We know this is so, because You have shown us many times in many ways that this is true. Thank you! Thank you!

BE KIND TO YOURSELF

Talk to yourself like you would talk to someone you love. - Brené Brown

Imagine that you are getting dressed for work and that you remember today is the day of the office party. You are supposed to dress festively and bring a treat. You didn't buy a Santa tie or jingle-bell earrings. If you are like most people, you are saying, "I'm such a knucklehead! I forgot to buy some festive accessories. Plus, I forgot to bake a treat for the holiday party. Dumb, dumb, dumb!"

Am I right?

If one of your coworkers called you and related the same tale of woe, you most likely would say, "Drive by the big-box store on your way to work. They have racks of silly accessories, and their bakery is open all night. Put the treats on your own plate, and no one will know the difference."

Right, again?

So why are we more kind to our friends than to ourselves? We are perfectionists, we have family expectations...there could be any number of reasons. By perfectionism, I don't mean doing our best, and if it's not quite right, do it again. I'm talking about a mind-set that tells us we are the lowest of the low if everything we do isn't perfect and praise-worthy. As for family expectations, well, your mother isn't going to be at the party, so you don't have to impress her.

I'm challenging you to spend 24 hours being as nice to yourself as you are to your family, friends, coworkers and strangers. "Oh, that's easy," you say. Is it? Keep a note pad in your pocket, and each time you criticize yourself, make a notation. You don't have to write down what you said to yourself or why. Just make a dot or check mark. At the end of the day, count the marks.

Learning to be as kind to yourself as you are to others can be a big project. So tackle this goal like any other big project. Do a little each day, and congratulate yourself on each improvement.

155

Being nice to yourself is especially important this time of year. Society piles more expectations on us this season than during any other month: parties, gifts with beautiful wrappings, cheerfulness, homemade treats, concerts, school plays and on and on. We try to live up to those expectations and find ourselves feeling overwhelmed and maybe a bit angry at ourselves for falling into the holiday rush, when we'd really like to sit at home with a cup of cocoa or glass of wine and watch "Miracle on 34th Street" for the 40th time.

Why not give yourself the gift of serenity this year? Can we look at the list of events on our calendar and choose to attend only those that we'll enjoy?

Spirit, we thank you that we have so many reasons to celebrate. We enjoy celebrating, but we also know that we often fill our calendars with so many events that we feel overwhelmed rather than joyful. We choose to spend this month being joyful rather than resentful.

WATCH FOR CHANGE

"I've said it before, and I'll say it again: The way to start changing your mind is not to force it or command it, but to watch it."
-Martha Beck

Motivational speakers, life coaches and our parents, tell us that if we want to do something, we need to make a decision to do it, and then do it. This is the path to success.

But, is it?

For some Type-A people, yes. For the rest of us, not so much. We decide to go to the gym every day. We go for about a week. Then it's less and less often until we realize that we haven't been to the gym for three months and our gym bag is buried under the dirty laundry hamper.

Have you ever noticed yourself making changes just by thinking it might be a nice thing to do?

One easy example is food. When I was growing up, I'd watch my parents enjoy cottage cheese and grapefruit. They would offer it to me knowing that they'd receive a one-word response: "Yuck!" Years later I was offered a tasty, fruity dish. I asked for the recipe. Imagine my surprise when she said the main ingredient was cottage cheese! My mind was changed not by determining that I would like cottage cheese, but by just allowing it to flow into my world. The same happened with grapefruit.

On the other hand, my parents ate a lot of liver. That came about when my mother was young and severely anemic. Her doctor told her, "Eat it cooked now or raw later." Because her survival was the goal, determination worked.

When I was old enough, they forced me to eat it too. Since I was healthy, my motivation was not survival; rather, it was being allowed to leave the table. I couldn't hide a sliver of liver in enough mashed potatoes or green beans to disguise its taste and texture. The moment I left home, I determined never to eat liver again, and I never did - except once:

My love took me to a fancy restaurant for my Valentine's Day birthday. The ambiance was pure romance: dim lighting, table candles, linen, silver, crystal, and subtle, romantic music. The waiter brought a multi-tiered Lazy Susan stacked with a variety of creamy, tempting treats and tiny crackers. I sampled this treat and that one, enjoying their tastes and textures when my date said, "This one is really good. Try it."

So I did and, "YUCK! LIVER!" burst forth before I could stop myself. Every face in the restaurant turned my way, showing clear distain for the peasant who couldn't control herself in public.

This kind of automatic conditioning applies in almost every situation. Just accepting that a co-worker is cranky and allowing him or her to be that way makes life easier for both of you. But one day discovering the reason for their crankiness may bring a change of attitude.

This also works for exercise, learning a new skill, or even getting up to go to work each morning. I'm not suggesting that we'll learn to love everything, but relaxing, accepting and watching will change our attitudes and our actions, often before we realize it.

Spirit, thank you for this lovely, cool day, a good day to do something productive. We can determine to finish a certain project and feel frustrated when this or that interruption prevents us from meeting our goals. On the other hand, we can accept the day as it unfolds, watching what happens and becoming happily surprised that a more important change has occurred in us, seemingly without effort. You have promised us that if we let life flow, miracles will happen.

WHAT NOW?

"...The important question is not 'Why me?' but 'What now?'...perhaps picking ourselves up, moving on, and learning what it is we're called to do with our lives." -Beverly Donofrio*

This quote is a reminder of where our thoughts should take us. So many of us grew up with "why me?" on the tips of our tongues. We hauled it out for all occasions: chemistry tests, bad relationships, terrible jobs, and nosy neighbors. The list could go on for pages, but we all know which disasters we rationalize. Whatever happens is never our fault. We're innocent victims upon whom the Universe has chosen to dump the latest unpleasant event.

Years ago, I was having a "why me?" episode, whining about everything – job, kids, love life, bills, health, you name it. Fortunately, a wise woman became tired of listening to my woes and asked, "Why not you? What makes you so special that you don't need to experience the same life challenges as the rest of us?" I gasped at her audacity. How dare she say my terrible life was no worse than anyone else's?

What a wake-up call! After absorbing that blow to my dignity, I began listening more closely to the other women in our group instead of impatiently waiting for my turn to spew my unhappiness. She was right. The other women had lives equally bad or worse than mine.

At that point I had to shift to the second part of the quote, "What now?" The immediate "what now" was to shut up, listen and learn.

"Why me?" keeps us living as victims of our limiting beliefs. But when we shift to "What now?" we start to see options. We have an opportunity to evaluate the situation and decide what step will move us into that new space.

Recently my workplace instituted a new hiring and benefit system. I didn't go to "Why me?" because I knew that all employees were facing the same situation. However, I got stuck on "What now?" This led to fretting and trying to make an immediate decision. Fortunately, a friend reminded me that I didn't need to make a decision that day or even that week. I had several months to consider options.

So the lesson is not to get stuck on any of these levels. "What now?" is a much better place to be than "Why me?" but it can be a stumbling block too. We need to remember that "Why me?" is a trap and "What now?" is a stepping stone to a new adventure.

Spirit, we thank you for these lessons and opportunities. We know that we are not stuck in a trap or on a step that imprisons us. We know that every change in our life experience (these happen almost every minute) can lead us in new, exciting directions. We know this is true, because you have promised it and have provided us with guides and angels to lead us on our life path. As long as we listen to our guides, whether human or from the other side, we will move forward with enthusiasm and joy.

*From an interview in the June, 2013 issue of "O, the Oprah magazine."

CREATE YOUR REALITY

"Life isn't about finding yourself. Life is about creating yourself." -George Bernard Shaw

Most of us live our lives backward. We think that we are empty vessels who need to find our purpose somewhere out there. If we look hard enough to find something that resonates with us and follow that path, we find ourselves.

Some of us are fortunate enough to know from childhood what we are meant to do. Those lucky people can focus their energies on going to the right schools to prepare for their future, and the rest falls into place.

Many of us tend to wander through life hoping to find which career or person will make us happy. We admire those who have definite goals and wish that we were so certain. We stumble into careers and/or family situations that may or may not fill our yearning. Each time we fail, we get more downhearted and ask God for a sign.

I used to say, "God, please show me a giant neon sign with a flashing arrow that says, 'Go this way, Stupid.'"

Well, God never did give me a neon sign. Rather, I learned in subtler ways what path was right for me. He gave me three wonderful children and two husbands who weren't quite so wonderful. But every person, even non-family members, was in my life for a reason. Their purpose was to show me what I did and didn't want. Similarly, I had to learn which career paths were right and wrong for me.

Some of us never learn those lessons and keep stumbling throughout our lives. Others of us are slow learners, but we eventually decipher the code and realize that life really isn't a puzzle. Instead, life is a series of paths, all of which are right to teach us what we need to know in a particular situation. Even when we walk on what seems the wrong path, it curves back to the right path. I once read that the right path appears sparkly, and the wrong one (actually the longer path) appears dark.

If we sincerely desire to live life on our terms, eventually we become able to see the sparkles. At first the sparkles are dim. Each time we follow the path to our dreams, the sparkles get brighter until we can no longer doubt we are on the right path.

Once we get to that point we realize we didn't find our reality; we created it.

God, Spirit, Higher Power, Creator: Thank you for this awareness. We cheerfully shed our belief that we have to find our way through life. As we shed that old paradigm, we put on a cloak of creating ourselves, our lives, and our futures. Whatever we create is always right. As long as we follow our truth, life will be exactly right for us. We know this is so, because this is the message that has come to us through many generations of holy teachers.

SPIRITUAL HELP IS LIKE MAGIC

"…Where our attention goes, so go our lives." -Martha Beck

I work in a magic shop in a theme park, and, as often as possible, I watch the magician perform his tricks. I'm always impressed by his ability to make things appear and disappear at will. It seems like the object at hand has simply vanished. But has it? Not really. The magician waves his magic wand or wiggles his fingers and suddenly the object appears again. He directs our attention to one hand while the other one is performing the trick.

Watching him day after day has made me think of God/Spirit/Higher Power (or whatever you choose to call the entity you petition when you have a problem). Sometimes we go through life not giving our spiritual life much thought. We simply go along day by day knowing the next day will be the same as the last. Then, one day, catastrophe strikes. We lose our job. A loved one falls ill with a debilitating disease. A family member crosses over to the heavenly side of life. We wonder why this horrible event has happened to us. We wonder where our Mother/Father God has gone. Why has God deserted us in this time of need?

Our spiritual guidance has not disappeared. Our attention has been diverted. We have been looking at our electronic gadgets, the food in front of us, or our daily tasks, and we have not been looking where God really is: in a friend's smile, in the sweet-smelling magnolia blossom, in a baby's eyes, and (even closer to home) in our hearts. All we need to do is to look in the right place, and, just as we see the magical object reappear, we will see our Higher Guidance right in front of us.

Spirit, today I choose to be in peace, love, and joy. I choose that everyone with whom I come into contact is in peace, love and joy. I choose to be present, aware, and in the moment. I comprehend, integrate, and communicate all that You present to me today.

163

BE QUIET AND LISTEN

"I bet God that if I lived, I would try to find out the vague directions whispered in my ears and find the road it seemed I must follow." Zora Neale Hurston*

Finding our path in life often seems an endless struggle. Few of us are fortunate enough to know from an early age where our destination lies. The rest of us struggle to hear "the vague directions whispered" in our ears. How do we know which thoughts are ours and which are God's?

For years I would exclaim in frustration, "God, please put a neon sign in front of my face that says 'This way, Stupid' with a giant arrow pointing the way." While seeking the sign, I wandered from this situation to that, only to realize those were not the right paths for me. Eventually, someone wiser than I told me to stop looking for the neon sign and listen to the quiet voice in my head. Great advice, but not an easy task.

First, we need to quiet the outside noise that fills our daily lives: television, movies, the lawnmower outside, the neighbor's barking dog, a co-worker's radio playing programs we don't like. Some of those things we can take action to correct. Others we just have to accept and put them in their proper perspective.

Second, we need to quiet our own minds enough to hear that voice. That is more difficult: bills to pay, family needs, overly-full schedule, housework, yard work, not enough sleep. Still, we can and must quiet our internal racket by asking our Higher Power to keep us focused on the task at hand while letting those distractions just float in one ear and out the other side. We can give our brains permission to not grasp those things until we need to consider them.

Third, we have to learn which thoughts come from Spirit and which come from our ego. Ego-thoughts are usually centered on showing the other person who's better, nicer, prettier; or they may be focused on getting even or making more money. Spirit-directed thoughts center on what will make us happy, what will help other people, and what will draw us closer to our God. When we get to that point, life is beautiful and we know our path.

The challenge is staying centered in that way, realizing that our emotions are a part of us and intended to keep us on our path. Anger, jealousy, and envy are all just emotions that do not require action. We must decide if acting on them will lead us further down our path or divert our attention and send us another way. Our history is filled with many examples of men and women who channeled their emotions constructively. Can we follow their examples, or will we allow our emotions to lead us away from our path?

That is a question we will face many times in our lives. Each choice will determine our path. What choice is right for you?

Fourth and last, remember the bumpy times with gratitude. They teach us what doesn't work, and we make some friends along the way.

*Zora Neale Hurston was talking about her recovery period in a free ward at a New York City hospital after appendicitis surgery. At that time recovering from appendicitis was an iffy affair.

WATCH YOUR THOUGHTS

"Monitor your thoughts carefully, and be sure to only think about what you want, not what you don't want…the universe has just taken a snapshot of your thoughts and is manifesting them into form. Are you pleased with what thoughts the universe has captured? If not, correct your thoughts." Doreen Virtue, Healing with the Angels

I'm sharing a crystal clear example of Virtue's wisdom that was given to me this week. Hopefully, you'll learn by example rather than the way I did.

This past week was evidence that Murphy's Law is still alive and working hard. I felt overwhelmed by all I had to do to get ready for the many projects on my calendar. I worried that I wouldn't get it all done. I was correct. I wasn't able to get my tasks finished, and I felt unprepared to meet the rest of the week. I had manifested my thoughts and fears.

At least I'm not sitting here wondering what went wrong. The Universe made the message loud and clear: "You manifested your thoughts. Do you like what you received?" I did not like what I received, except for these benefits: the message I needed to hear and the fact that I was able to laugh at my foolishness and relax.

Since I did that, everything that has to be done is getting done. Other projects are delayed until next week when I can give them my full attention.

Not only did the universe manifest my thoughts and fears, it also slowed the various activities to a manageable level. This is what I needed, not what I imagined I wanted.

Spirit, I'm grateful for this opportunity to learn how to manifest what I don't want as well as what I do want. I appreciate the clear lesson that was easy to understand. I am grateful for all the teachers I've had who prepared me to understand this lesson when it came. I know that what I learned this week will stay with me, because you have said that it is so. With joy, I confirm that it is so!

BE WHO YOU ARE NOW

"The most inspirational thing about Don is that … his age is irrelevant…His age doesn't keep him from doing anything he wants to do…I think women should aim to age that way." Gabrielle Reece

Today's quote is from the May, 2013, issue of "O, The Oprah Magazine." Reece was talking about aging in general and her friend, Don, in particular. Don is 80 years old and is still running marathons, surfing and snowboarding. Reece explores this topic in greater detail in her book, *My Foot is too Big for the Glass Slipper.*

I love that title. It says that we are neither Cinderella nor Prince Charming. We are real women and men who are often reluctant to live our lives to the fullest for a variety of reasons. We let other people give us false expectations of whom we should be, ignoring the fact that we're not all Cinderella or Prince Charming. In the process, we bury our real selves and live lives according to society's rules, not realizing that the people whom we admire most have broken those rules and have lived lives according to their inner promptings.

Earlier this week I was listening to a cd recording of a "Science of Mind" class taught by Rev. Angela Peregoff. She reminded her class that not all restrictions come from our parents and teachers. She told the story of becoming lethargic after her 50th birthday. She contacted her guides and asked them why her energy level had dropped so suddenly and that she just didn't want to make the effort to reach her goals.

Rev. Angela's guides showed her a previous life in which women were considered old at 50. They were expected to sit around drinking tea and to take a lot of naps. She told her guides that she honored that lifetime, but she didn't want to live according to those rules during this lifetime. By facing her history and honoring it, Rev. Angela was able to put those rules behind her and continue following her current lifetime's path.

Hearing that immediately sent me back to the times my mother would say to me, "You're retired now. Why are you still working?

Why are you expending your energy instead of relaxing?" While I only bought about half of that statement, the half I did buy into set obstacles in my path. When I plan this or that adventure, I get sick, rain falls for days at a time, or I'm just so tired all I can do is nap. All are good excuses to sit in my recliner wishing, instead of training for an adventure or even going to the library to get books about what I can expect to see when I journey.

These two teachers, Rev. Angela and my mother, have inspired me to move beyond what has been expected of me. I can no longer use age as an excuse.

God, I'm asking you and my guides to move me gently, yet firmly, into a more active lifestyle. I know you gave me life so that I can live it to the fullest. I trust that with your guidance I can move into a more productive life filled with adventures and love. I know this is so, because you have promised it in your holy word.

EXPECTATIONS

"If you are always trying to be normal you will never know how amazing you can be." -Maya Angelou*

"Life can only be understood backward; but it must be lived forwards." -Soren Kierkegaard*

Life is filled with contradictions. Last week I was filled with despair because I felt I did not live up to certain alumnae expectations. Of course, by the time I finished journaling my sob-story, the despair was gone. Just putting the words on paper gave my thoughts structure and evaporated the power of the anxiety that flew around hitting this nerve or that sore spot in my mind.

Today's quotes put that angst and recovery in perspective. I am not, and never will be, normal (whatever that is). Only by looking back can I understand how amazing was graduating college at the age of forty-seven.

I began life born with a full head of bright red hair on Valentine's Day. That put me in the not-normal category before I had done anything more interesting than burp! Since my mother had brown hair and my father had white-blonde hair, the predominant question the rest of my childhood was, "Where did she get that red hair?" The naturally related comment was, "Oh, you have so many freckles!" All this was happening when my goal was to get a tan like normal people. Covering up at the beach when everyone else was stretched out in the sand was misery.

The next not-normal thing that happened was my making the honor roll every year until I quit trying. My parents were children of the Depression. School was not high on many parents' priority list – food and work were the top issues. My parents did not lack intellectual ability; they just lacked education. So the second question was, "How did she get so smart?" I was proud of being smart but tired of the insinuations that my parents were dumb. Even I thought they were dumb until I was old enough to look back and see how much they had accomplished.

169

I could go on and on, but you get the idea. I was not considered normal by most adults or classmates. How I longed to be like everyone else! I'll just say that feeling alienated led me to make some "stupid" mistakes that ironically led to gifts like my children, travel, library cards in many locations, and unusual experiences.

Now that I've reached a mature age and have four great-grandchildren, the "other blonde" has softened the red in my hair. People are now aware of skin-cancer and the need to cover-up. So I look more normal. Thanks to public information and television shows like "Scorpion" and "Big Bang Theory" about people who have IQs much higher than mine, I'm considered normal, although I am an unusually young great-grandmother.

Now I can look back and understand that I've had an amazing life. I also have an amazing future to contemplate. What more can I ask of life? I thank Universal Energy for all the experiences that brought me to where I am today, even though they seemed difficult at the time.

*Both quotes are from "Inspiration, 5-7-15 Defy Ordinary" by Pamela Harper, www.pamelaharper.com

WE ARE ENOUGH

"If we have to seek approval from others to accept our own choices, then we already made the wrong choice." -Window of Wisdom*

A few days ago, I wrote about accepting or not another's behavior and fretting about what they are doing. Today I'm going to approach the same topic from a different angle – our own.

We know instinctively what is best for us, so why do we seek another's advice before taking action? Perhaps it is the way we were raised, or maybe our decisions were devalued as adults. Possibly we were told so many times that we couldn't make a decision if our lives depended upon it that we came to believe it. How we arrived at this dependent behavior doesn't matter. What matters is what we choose to do about it.

Do we continue relying on our friends and relatives to advise our decisions, or do we just jump in, make a decision, and live with the results? If we jump in, it is most likely that our decision will be confirmed in any number of ways.

I must admit that, after many years of learning to make my own choices, I started to slip back into indecision. A situation arose that had me stuck. I knew what to do, but I feared the feedback from others. This lack of confidence made me question my ability to decide. My indecision led me to write a rambling email to a friend asking for advice. Just as I prepared to send the email, my computer froze and the email was lost.

Losing that email made me realize that the decision was mine and only mine and that I had no business asking my friend to become involved in my problem.

I wrote my friend another email saying that I had a difficult decision to make and would tell him what I planned when I made it. After sleeping on the problem, I still feared the responses I might receive, but I took the necessary action and began to breathe easier. Imagine my surprise when I received emails from several people saying that they approved my choice!

171

I am grateful for this gentle reminder that I need to make my own decisions. Practicing small decisions gives me the confidence to make the right choices when the stakes are much larger, as they can be as we age. I find that there are times to rely on my daughters. In other situations, I don't require their advice. If I lean on them too much, they may begin to worry that I am losing my capacity to make good decisions.

*" Window 787," by awindowofwisdom@wordpress.com

EXPRESS GRATITUDE

"The art of acceptance is the art of making someone who has done you a small favor wish that he might have done you a greater one." Russel Lynes[1]

Gratitude is not just to be felt, but also to be expressed. Too often we feel grateful for someone who has done something nice for us, but we often do not express our gratitude. We say, "Thanks," or "Ok, nice," and let it go at that. Yet when we do something nice for others, we hope that they will express their thanks in a more effusive manner, such as, "Oh, what a wonderful thing you did! I really appreciate your hard work."

Often this happens because of the way we were raised. Erma Bombeck once wrote, "I'm going to call my dad to tell him I love him – and listen to him say, 'This call is costing you a fortune' and hang up."[2] My parents grew up during the Depression when people had very little money to buy gifts. As a result, when they received a gift or kindness, they often questioned the giver's ability to provide that gift. For example, my mother would usually say something like, "This is pretty, but it costs too much." This is not quite as curt as Erma Bombeck's dad, but the words still hurt.

Six or seven years ago, I felt so frustrated that I said, "Mom, you take all the fun out of giving." She responded, "My friend recently told me that I take the blessing out of giving." I replied that her friend was right. Mom became somewhat more expressive of her gratitude after that.

An excellent example of this happened when I was in high school. My church's youth group planned a spring break trip to New York City. I saved up as much money as I could, and my parents added the rest, even though it stretched their budget to the limit. A few days before the trip, my geometry teacher asked me to stay after class. My imagination saw all sorts of terrible situations. When class was over, I reluctantly made my way to her desk only to learn that she was gifting me with $20 to spend however I wished on the trip. While on the trip, I budgeted carefully, did not spend the $20, and purchased a $1 or $2 souvenir for her to express my gratitude. My parents congratulated me on my frugality.

On my first day back to school, I presented the teacher with the trinket and she thanked me. Pleased with her gratitude, I gave her the $20 and told her I didn't need it. With a sad face, she responded, "I know you didn't need it, but I wanted you to enjoy yourself a little more than your budget would allow." I didn't understand the impact of returning the money until much later. I was an ungrateful receiver of her kindness. My pride had not let me spend her generous gift.

As I look back, I realize how much I hurt her feelings. I know that I cannot make amends since she has long since left earthly life. The only way I can repay her kindness is to do as Anne Morrow Lindbergh said, "One can never pay in gratitude; one can only pay 'in kind' somewhere else in life."[3]

I ask my Guides to remind me more often of all that has been lovingly given and to pay it forward as often as I can.

[1] Reader's Digest 1954, listed in The New Penguin Dictionary of Modern Quotations
[2] Treasury of Women's Quotations, pg. 67, Carolyn Warner, Prentice Hall
[3] Treasury of Women's Quotations, pg. 144, Carolyn Warner, Prentice Hall

Chapter Seven: Holidays

HAPPY NEW YEAR...OR IS IT?

Einstein and other prominent scientists, as well as many spiritual leaders, have explained that all time is simultaneous. If time is simultaneous, then we have no new year to celebrate. I have no wish to "harsh your mellow." If you wish to celebrate the new year, go for it. Parties are fun, and what better excuse than a perceived new year?

Then I recall the simultaneous thing and realize that I was here when the Earth was formed. I was here when pyramids were built. I was here when the United States became an independent nation. And I was present at my high school graduation. I've always been here – and so have you. What an empowering thought!

I'm not sure I understand this time concept, but I know it changed my thoughts about things like New Year's Day. I enjoy every moment of preparing for birthday and holiday celebrations. I wonder how time can be simultaneous when I can see my great-grandsons growing seemingly minute by minute, or I look in the mirror and see wrinkles and gray hair that wasn't there twenty years ago. This seems to be proof that time is continuous. If time was simultaneous, I wouldn't age. Or would I?

We've earned our wrinkles and gray hair. I often wish I'd remember what I learned during those long ago years. However, I also know that I don't want to recall the catastrophic events.

Don't giggle, you beautiful young men and women. You'll arrive here someday and wonder where the years have gone. How did your babies become grandparents? Where did your bikini body go?

Time is simultaneous, but our lives have beginnings and ends, then begin and end again and again. We never really die; rather, we move to a different dimension to learn what we need to know for our next human lifetime. There is a reason we don't recall who we were before. It might affect how we respond to certain events. Our goal is to react according to what we know at the moment, not what we knew a thousand years ago.

Now, let's get back to the pending New Year's Eve that leads into a new year. Enjoy it to the fullest no matter your circumstances. If you happen to be alone, do something that will make you happy. Watch a silly movie or a football game. Read a book that has been on your to-do list for many years. Eat some popcorn and drink a soda, or be classy and enjoy cheese and wine. Play Monopoly by yourself. You're sure to win. You'll take that win with you the rest of your days.

HAPPY NEW YEAR! Peace, love and joy will be with you every moment of this new year.

Creator Spirit, thank you for giving us knowledge and the willingness to live in peace, love and joy each day, no matter what those days bring. Just knowing that You have always been here to guide us and teach us what we need to know to live each day to the fullest.

NEW YEAR

"Time is not at all what it seems. It does not flow in only one direction, and the future exists simultaneously with the past." -Albert Einstein, physicist.

Dr. Einstein understood things differently than most of us. We can understand his reasoning on a higher mental level, but we don't understand and experience it in our daily lives. We can't comprehend the thought that our life today is happening at the exact same moment as the cave people began building houses, the pyramids were built, or even Christmas morning – the first one and the one we just experienced.

"Time is what prevents everything from happening at once." John Wheeler, physicist.

Since we are humans having human experiences, we look at time like John Wheeler. We experience each day individually, which is useful in getting to work on time or just trying to remember where we are supposed to be and what we should be doing at any particular minute.

Have you ever had the feeling that you are supposed to be two places at once? Have you ever been in a normal situation but wondering why you are there and what you are supposed to do? Have you ever been in a new location/situation, yet feeling like you've been there before? Those mini-events are hints that we are experiencing time simultaneously.

However, since everyone reading this message is a human living a human experience, I will wish you a "HAPPY NEW YEAR!"

Spirit, we thank you for the year that just passed and all the people and events in our lives. We perceived some as good and some as bad. We know that you give us experiences to teach us what we need to know to move to our next life event. We know that all experiences are good and we need to pay attention to what is happening to us and around us so we will be prepared. Thank you for those lessons and the knowledge that we experience time both simultaneously and sequentially.

DR. MARTIN LUTHER KING, JR. DAY

"Darkness cannot drive out darkness: only light can do that. Hate cannot drive out hate: only love can do that." Dr. Martin Luther King, Jr.

Recently, we celebrated Dr. King's birthday, each in our own way. Some went to memorial services or marched a few blocks to recall the difficult times of the 1960s. Others used the three-day weekend to go skiing. Some ignored the whole event. How did you celebrate or not? I used the time to complete some tasks at home while thinking about how my life has been impacted by this man's teachings.

Opinions about Dr. King's legacy vary, but not as widely as they did when he was prodding the United States' conscience. I have heard him be called a leader, peacemaker, hatemonger and communist (the ultimate epithet of the 1960s). I heard rants when he was awarded the Nobel Peace Prize. I was not a part of the Movement, just a watcher, but I have my own thoughts about that time. I hope you'll indulge my memories and reflect on how your life has changed since Dr. King's time on Earth.

One summer my family traveled south in our rattle-trap car to visit relatives. At one point, I had severe urgencies. My dad stopped at a gas-station with outdoor facilities. The white restroom was closed for repairs. I ran to the other one and was turned away by a kind black woman who told me I would need to go down the street a few blocks to another gas station. If she let me inside, she would lose her job. This made no sense. A bathroom was a bathroom and I needed one *immediately*.

At church I was learning about the dignity of all God's creatures, but I was seeing cruelty and hate on television. I saw bus boycotts, marches and sit-ins, fire hoses, church bombings, police dogs attacking marchers, and masses of people crammed into tiny jail cells. These sights and sounds found a home in my mind.

I did not participate in any of these activities, but I watched with a heavy heart. As a teen at home, my parents feared for my safety

179

and forbade me to participate. Later as a young wife, I did not participate because I feared that an arrest would mean a pay-grade reduction for my Army husband.

Then 1968 arrived, and I thought the end of the world had arrived with it. We experienced the Tet Offensive in Vietnam, Dr. King's assassination, riots and shootings, Robert Kennedy's assassination, and more riots and shootings. I was terrified. I "knew" this was the end. Just as television news terrified me, television also saved my sanity by airing the irreverent "Smothers Brothers Show" and Rowan and Martin's "Laugh-in."

Many years later when I worked for The Madison Times, I had the opportunity to interview Dr. James Jones, who watched Dr. King's "I Have a Dream Speech" from his office window while drafting the Civil Rights Act of 1964. Not long after that, Shirley Chisholm, the first black woman to run for Congress, granted an interview for the same paper. They were both gracious and kind to this white woman who sat on the sidelines during the movement's worst days.

Even now, events occur that lead to riots and marches. We've come a long way but have a long way to go. We see interethnic strife not just in our country, but around the world. Attacks and murders by militants who think everyone should believe as they do are becoming all too commonplace.

I understand that as humans we are contentious creatures who tend to believe that someone needs to be the lead dog and that it should be ME. However, we need to remember the words not only of Dr. King, but also of other leaders: Jesus, crucified; Gandhi, assassinated; and the Dalai Lama, forced from his homeland.

For a different perspective, we can remember comedian Flip Wilson, who portrayed on television, Geraldine, a character whose catch-phrase was, "What you see is what you get!" We laughed and adopted the phrase as our own. Later I realized that, along with Flip, the leaders I mentioned were saying that if you expect hatred, you will experience hatred. If you practice love, you will receive love many times over what you expect.

Those people gained notoriety and fame for teaching peace. More commonly, we internalize what we learn from those close to us: family, friends, and people we meet. I've learned that even though the news constantly bombards us with violence and hatred, most people I meet are kind. I see love in their eyes. Occasionally, I see fear, but a soft voice and kind actions turn the fear into appreciation.

Do you choose to see darkness or light?

VALENTINE'S DAY

"… Show them love not once a year but on any Tuesday. Tell them. Be kind. Be patient. Treat them with tenderness. Keep your heart soft and keep it open…" Molly Dugger Brennan

This week we are inundated with reminders to buy gifts for our romance partners. Everywhere we go we see displays of flowers, candy, jewelry, and nightwear with hearts all over it. The message is buy, buy, buy love or, at least, romance for an evening.

This morning I was touched when I read Dugger Brennan's blog, "Share the Love".[1] She talked about real love between her and her family. I had to agree. We don't tell the people in our lives how much we appreciate them, except on special days, and sometimes not then.

I'm expanding her definition of loved ones to all who share our lives: relatives, neighbors, mail carriers, newspaper carriers, store clerks…you know the list. We don't have to get all gushy. A smile and a thank you will make their day. By the way, how often do we smile and thank the people who share our homes? Or do we just assume they'll always be there, bugging us to keep our feet off the furniture and eat our broccoli?

Abraham/Hicks[2] talks frequently about a "Rampage of Appreciation," a simple way to make life more pleasant and welcome new experiences. As we go through our day, we can notice little things that make life pleasant. For example: Tulips are blooming. Someone emptied the trash. The newspaper is on the sidewalk for a change. A favorite shirt is clean. Not much traffic on the interstate today. Each time we notice and appreciate something, we notice more and more things that please us. Pretty soon we're smiling a lot more than we did yesterday or last week.

This is not suggesting that we disregard unpleasant events. Our child is ill. Of course, we are concerned and taking necessary steps to make him or her feel better. At the same time, we can remember what a precious gift that child is and smile. We can be thankful for health insurance and a car that takes us to the drug store for medicine.

I'll stop here. If I continue, we might all die of an overdose of sweetness. Even so, please, let's remember to show our gratitude and pleasure in the small things in life. Everything goes better with a smile.

Spirit, thank you for this day. Thank you for the opportunity to tell the people in our lives that we love and care for them. Thank you for the opportunity to see and hear all the wonderful things happening in our world. Thank you that we are alive and able to enjoy life as it occurs. Even the people or events that we wish were gone have gifts to offer. We ask you to make apparent to us those gifts so that we can appreciate all in our world.

[1] http://blog.mollyduggerbrennan.com, "Share the Love," February 12, 2014

[2] "The Teachings of Abraham," Esther and Jerry Hicks

EARTH DAY

"Sometimes, I laugh so hard, it starts a hurricane in the heavens. Sometimes, I grin so wide, it causes earthquakes on distant planets. And, sometimes, when I feel so happy I could float, worlds are born, continents rise, and oceans surge. But never, ever, ever, do I lay so much as a finger on planet Earth. Because there, my work is long over, and yours has just begun... Trust me, this barely hints of your true power...." The Universe*

Today is Earth Day, and this quote is apropos to its significance. I'm not going to lecture you on recycling, driving a smaller car, or wearing a bicycle helmet. Rather, I'm going to talk about something even more important to the future of our Earth – each of us as individuals.

For me, the key lines in this quote are, "But never, ever, ever, do I lay so much as a finger on planet Earth. Because there, my work is long over, and yours has just begun."

Where do we start doing that work? Being kind to others? Yes. Being kind to animals? Yes. Planting trees? Yes. However, before we can do those things, we must first take care of ourselves.

"But...but...but," you say. I say there are no "buts." We MUST take care of ourselves first. How can we raise compassionate, responsible children if we do not treat ourselves compassionately and responsibly? How can we treat other people and animals kindly if we don't do the same for ourselves? We must take time to relax. We must stop and watch a sunset. We must watch a movie that makes us laugh until we cry. Only by taking care of ourselves first can we take adequate care of those for whom we are responsible. We must be sure that we are strong, healthy, and well rested in order to provide for those we love and, by extension, our community and our Earth. Enough lecture. I hope your Earth Day is beautiful and happy and that you smile all day.

*TUT – A Note from the Universe, April 20, 2015, aka Mike Dooley, www.tut.com

MEMORIAL DAY

"Patriotism is merely a religion – love of country, worship of country, devotion to the country's flag, honor and welfare." -Samuel Clemens (Mark Twain)

A grateful thank you to all men and women who have served our country in times of war and peace is due every single day, not just on Memorial Day and Veteran's Day. We must also extend gratitude to those who waited at home for their loved ones to return, hopefully the same strong young men and women who left to defend their country or protect another country's right to exist. Honor all those who have answered their nation's call in whatever ways that they could: Victory Gardens, assisting their neighbors, prayers for safety.

At the same time, I yearn for the day we no longer hear those calls. Are we humans capable of living in peace? I think of songs we sing in church and contemplate their confusing messages: "Onward Christian Soldiers" and "I Ain't Going to Study War No More."

All religions teach peace. Often we greet each other by bowing and saying, "Namaste," or, "The sacred in me greets the sacred in you." Even shaking hands indicates that our hands hold no weapons. These behaviors are ingrained into our daily lives, yet we forget or disregard the meaning behind them. Is this dichotomy the reason so many of our returning veterans are committing suicide? We send them to war. The next day they are at home and are expected to act like the horror never happened. We can't forget violence in twenty-four hours.

Spirit, mixed messages about peace and war assault us on all sides. On one hand, we talk about war to impose peace. On the other, we see the damage war has caused to the minds and hearts of all involved. Our holy books teach us peace. We ask that you implant a stronger desire for peace than we have for dissension.

WINTER HOLIDAYS

"One of the most essential tasks for living a life of purpose and joy is to command your time, rather than let it command you." - Martha Beck*

Beck said it so well. In this age of doing more with less and over-scheduling ourselves with work, family and community demands, we tend to live by the clock. As a result, we feel constantly pressed for time. We feel that there is just not enough time in the day to do what we want to do. And, if you're like me, you're thinking, "Where did this year go? It's almost Christmas. Did we even have a summer?" It seems that every year gets shorter, or is that my imagination?

Today is a day of reflection on the sacrifices our veterans and their families have made for each of us. We need to take some time to thank those we can and reflect on the contributions of those who have gone before. Regrettably, many of us look at the calendar and say, "Today is Veteran's Day. That means the banks are closed. Darn, I should have gone yesterday." That makes this day just another time issue.

Remember the old saying, "Take time to smell the roses." As trite as it has become, those words hold a lot of truth. While we must give adequate time and energy to our jobs and commitments, we can do a lot more rose smelling.

We can take a moment to listen to what our child is telling us. We can take a moment to listen to the birds sing or watch a leaf float to the ground. We can take a moment to deeply enjoy that first sip of coffee, inhale the aroma, feel the warmth on our lips, hold the taste on our tongues, experience the warmth spreading throughout our bodies, and notice the alertness coming to our eyes and ears.

Do we envy the person who is over-worked? Do we envy the person whose stress level is fifteen minutes short of a stroke or heart attack? Of course not. We envy the people who command their time, finding moments to regenerate their lives and their souls.

Each of us can take a moment to be grateful for our own existence and the people in them. We can even be grateful that we have events in our lives that make us think that we are too busy to take a moment to express that gratitude. A quick "Thank you" tossed out in the midst of our busy-ness will reach its target and be acknowledged.

Spirit, thank you for this new day. Show me how to use each moment wisely. I choose to be the highest and best I can be this day.

* Daily Inspiration, Martha Beck, November 11, 2015
info@marthabeck.com

RELAXING IN THE WINTER HOLIDAYS

"The best way to create more free time is to take it. There isn't anyone who can give it to you. Not even me." -The Universe*

What a busy time of year this is! We are bustling around baking cookies for some event or going to a concert. We're trying to finish our holiday shopping or even hoping to start it in the next few days. We're cleaning the house for guests and putting up holiday decorations.

We worry if we should say, "Merry Christmas" or "Happy Holidays" to be more inclusive of other faiths. We examine our budgets to learn what we can buy this year and for whom to buy. We may just shop using our credit cards, having decided to defer our worries until January. Whatever we are doing, we are often doing it until we are stressed. One song tells us, "It's the hap-happiest time of the year." Let's be honest. Is that what we're really feeling?

Many of us are feeling stressed. We need a breather. Life isn't going to hand us a day off from work. Even if it does, most of us will use it to accomplish other tasks. We need to decide that we will take some time for ourselves. It doesn't need to be a day of lounging at the spa. (That would be nice though, wouldn't it?)

Many stores play holiday music to get us in the shopping mode. We can pause in the toys, televisions, or tools to listen to "Carol of the Bells" and breathe easier for a few minutes. Three minutes of listening and breathing will refresh us more than we can imagine. If we try, we can find time to read a few pages in a book or walk around the neighborhood quietly and enjoy our neighbors' decorations.

Oprah summarized this thought when she said, "Whether you have a week to laze around or a 20-minute break between errands, I promise it is possible to relax." **

This is true. We have to be willing to delay a task; turn off the television, computer, and phone; go for a stroll; go to bed earlier; or make time to eat breakfast. The list goes on. We all have our own personal stressors and relaxers. Pick a relaxer that works for you and enjoy it.

Spirit, you designed us to live in balance for a good reason, yet most of us have too many stressors in our lives. Thank you for giving us tasks to keep us busy and also for time to relax and regenerate our minds and bodies so we can live in balance.

* theuniverse@tut.com, November 25, 2015
**"O, the Oprah Magazine," July, 2015

IT'S CHRISTMAS! LAUGH!

"We are never alone." Taylor Caldwell
"It seems to me at this moment that laughing is a serious thing, that it connects us with truth and love and God." -Martha Beck

Today is a day to celebrate. Many celebrate the birth of Jesus. Some celebrate other meaningful holidays. Outdoor people celebrate the opening of ski season. Tired people celebrate an opportunity to take a nap. It doesn't matter. Just pick a day, a season, and a reason to celebrate.

We celebrate laughing, as Martha Beck suggests. We celebrate never being alone, as Taylor Caldwell says. Even if we are physically alone, we are not truly alone. Everyone and everything in our Universe is connected.

Often we look at the news and think life is much too sad and violent to laugh. We must give this serious thought and try to find a solution. This is true. But we were created to laugh. Laughing clears the fear and allows our brains and our hearts to find a solution. Why else are so many of the holiday movies we watch year after year comedies?

So however you spend this day, no matter what sad event is happening, laugh!

The next message I write will come next year. Wow! That's a concept to laugh about!

Spirit, we thank you for the gift of never being alone. At times we feel so very sad and alone. Your universe is vast and filled with so many people, creatures and spirits that we can never truly be alone. We ask you to open our hearts to see those others and appreciate their presence. We thank you for the gifts of love and laughter and the ability to see that sometimes life is ridiculous and hilarious.

HOLIDAYS OF GREAT EXPECTATIONS

"Green is what I want to be. Be what you want to be." -Kermit the Frog

Winter holidays are times of great expectations (not Dickens' - the other kind: Christmas, Hanukkah, Kwanza, Dawili, and Winter Solstice). We have traditions that we feel compelled to continue. We want to show our best side to Great-Aunt Zelda, who criticizes everyone and everything. We try to convince our parents that the perfect marriage/job/new house is right around the corner. We've given up on our silly goal of being the next Ginger Rogers or Fred Astaire and have taken a job in an accounting firm. No dancing in the halls there!

To help us develop these expectations, we watch Christmas movies on television every evening, beginning a week or so before Thanksgiving. Even though each movie contains challenges for our hero or heroine, we know that in the end all will be perfect and that everyone will be thrilled with their family and gifts. Even Aunt Zelda has dipped in the punch bowl once too often and is singing a reggae version of Jingle Bells while dancing on the dining room table. Have you ever noticed that no one opens a gift of socks and that the new puppy doesn't poop on the floor in those movies?

Is there really any reason to tie ourselves into such knots? Why can't we just be who we are the rest of the year? Can't we be green every day?

Spirit, we thank you for the gifts you've given us throughout this year, even if that gift is a loss. We mourn the loss, but we know that all will work out for the good. We thank you that we don't have perfect families, because each crazy relative has a lesson for us. We thank you that this year we set spending limits for gifts. We thank you for all the reasons we have to celebrate, and we know that you want us to celebrate sanely.

MAKE QUIET IN THE WINTER HOLIDAYS

"Experience is not what happens to you, it is what you do with what happens to you." -Aldous Huxley

We are in the midst of several winter holidays, each with its individual traditions. Our families have expectations; our coworkers want gatherings; there are choir concerts, Christmas plays, shopping expeditions, and the search for the perfect tree. The list goes on and on.

Winter is naturally a time of rest. Just look out your window or take a walk in the woods. Leaves and nuts are on the ground, tree sap is in the roots, and most flowers are reserving their strength for spring and summer glory. Even in this area, we see fewer squirrels, birds and other woodland creatures. Some have gone underground until warm weather returns.

Traditionally, our own species used winter as a time of storytelling, creating crafts, and keeping warm. Without electric light, the days of our ancestors were short and nights were long. Christmas and New Year were times to see old friends and look forward to spring. They were also a time to remember years past and family members and friends who no longer sat at the dinner table. Sometimes those memories were joyful, and sometimes they were sad.

The quiet of winter is a good time to remember loved ones who have transitioned to a world free of pain. As much as we are glad they no longer feel pain, we miss their presence. Sometimes those who passed caused us much pain, and we feel relief that they are no longer in our lives. Either way, our pain remains. During the holidays those memories, good and bad, come back and sit with us until we acknowledge them.

Often we try to push the memories away by holiday busy-ness. That may work for a short time, but not for long. We must allow the memories to come forward, and we must feel the pain or joy that they bring.

We might take an hour or so to curl up in our recliners, cover ourselves with a soft blanket, and just remember and feel. Later, we can take several minutes to share our recent losses with a friend or a patient coworker. They will probably listen quietly and ask pertinent questions. It's amazing how much relief those two actions bring, especially if we feel overwhelmed by so many things to do and sad thoughts running through our heads at inconvenient times.

Please notice that even though we take time to honor those who are no longer here on Earth, this doesn't mean that we won't feel sad as we think of them. Rather, giving each a special time to honor their presence and absence will ease stress, making unexpected outbursts of grief or anger less likely to occur.

Some people use their grief to inform everyone within hearing distance of their sadness. Others sit quietly in their chairs all winter and grieve. Do you think your transitioned loved one wants you to wallow in the pain? Or do you think your loved one wants you to remember the good and bad times, and then go live your life?

Spirit, we thank you for memories. Thank you for the winter resting season. Thank you for guiding us to use the winter season for remembering and discerning the lessons of memories. Thank you for showing us how to remember past sad events without wallowing in our pain. We know that all things work together for the good of those who love.

THE SEASON OF PEACE AND GOODWILL

"Make your mind part of the world's peace, instead of its fear, and I promise, life will get better and better." -Martha Beck*

We're still wading through the winter holidays that continue through New Year's Day. We try to focus on a season of peace and goodwill, but we often get sidetracked and hit by the "winter blahs." At home, we might experience family dissension as we wash mounds of dishes in the kitchen. We growl to ourselves, "This is the season of joy, dammit!" We might experience lack...of everything. On the other hand, we might be lucky enough to share our bounty within a caring family.

Then, as the holidays wind to an end, we stop celebrating long enough to watch the news, and we see all the hate and violence occurring in our neighborhoods and around the world. We sigh and wonder if that can be changed or if we are doomed to live this way forever.

I can say without doubt - NO! Just as Beck says, if we set our minds on peace and act on that each day, our world will get better. I can hear you saying, "Yeah, right." However, it's true. When we think peace and kindness, we act on our beliefs, often not even aware that we are doing it. Each act will affect another person.

Remember the old shampoo commercial: if you tell two people, and they tell two people, then soon everyone will use this product. Just as word of mouth about shampoo will convince people to buy, our directed actions will eventually create peace. World peace probably will not happen anytime soon, but at least we can make our own little corner of the world a friendlier place.

I can see you shaking your head in doubt. "You don't know the jerks I have to deal with." I felt that way for many years. Then I became tired of feeling anger and stress and seeing it around me. I determined that I would create calm for myself. Each day when I get up, I state firmly, "I choose to be the best person I can be today." I find that by making that choice, my actions become kinder. As a result, I notice that people are kinder to me. That makes family life, friendships, and the work place kinder. I want to be with those people, instead of feeling obligated to be there.

Spirit, thank you for this beautiful day. Even if it's raining or snowing, the day is still beautiful. Thank you for knowing that if we become calm, life around us will become calm. Life can be wonderful, if we believe it to be so. We choose to act on that belief, knowing that all is happening for our highest good.

*Daily Inspiration, Martha Beck, December 25, 2015, info@marthabeck.com

About the Author

Echoes of Your Choices is Sharon Dillon's first book, hopefully to be followed by more. Over the years Sharon has been a reporter for several newspapers and magazines in both Wisconsin and Virginia. Writing on a deadline helped her quickly hone her skills. Now she writes to share what she has learned about living. Life, she believes, must be fun as well as serious and spiritual as well as practical. Through her blog of many years, "Thoughts to Ponder," Sharon shows that a wide angle lens is a must when viewing the world and the people who inhabit it.

Sharon has loved books since the first time her mother read her a story. Always providing her new subjects for learning and personal growth, books have been a staple of her life, bringing comfort, joy, shivers of fear, and a full range of emotions. She grew up in Ohio and has lived in many states, finally settling in Virginia after retiring from 25 years' employment with the State of Wisconsin. She now works part-time jobs that are fun at Busch Gardens Williamsburg and the Jamestown-Yorktown Foundation. Meeting new people daily provides her ideas for writing projects and expands her world view.

Sharon's writings are always about joy, peace and laughter. The most joyous times of Sharon's life are her individual play dates with four great-grandsons. She eagerly anticipates the birth of great-grandson number five. She is most proud of the wonderful adults her children have become. Her second most cherished achievement is having graduated from Alverno College in Milwaukee, WI, at the age of 47.

Sharon D. Dillon, author of "Twins! Oh, no!", one of 14 stories in *The Book of Mom: Reflections of Motherhood with Love, Hope and Faith*, published by booksyoucantrust.com. Available in print and e-format at Amazon.com.

Sharon is member of the Chesapeake Bay Writers, Erma Bombeck Writers Workshop, National Society of Newspaper Columnists, and Southern Humorists

Contact Sharon through e-mail at energywriter@cox.net.

Website: http://energywriter.me

Blog: "Thoughts to Ponder: Laugh your way to peace, love and joy."

www.ingramcontent.com/pod-product-compliance
Lightning Source LLC
Chambersburg PA
CBHW060238050426
42448CB00009B/1500